Recovery From Rescuing

Jacqueline Castine

Health Communications, Inc.
Deerfield Beach, Florida

Library of Congress Cataloging-in-Publication Data

Castine, Jacqueline
    Recovery from rescuing / Jacqueline Castine.
       p.   cm.
    Bibliography: p.
    ISBN 1-55874-016-3
    1. Co-dependence (Psychology)   I. Title.
  RC569.5.C63C37   1989
  158'.3—dc19

                                 88-32909
                                      CIP

© 1989 Jacqueline Castine
ISBN 1-55874-016-3

Published by Health Communications, Inc.
            Enterprise Center
            3201 Southwest 15th Street
            Deerfield Beach, FL 33442

Cover Design by Reta Thomas

Dedication

This book is dedicated to my children.

At great personal cost and inconvenience to themselves they lovingly, purposefully and persistently dedicated themselves to their roles of chemical dependency and irresponsibility until I learned the lessons they came into my life to teach me.

To John: Thank you for teaching me that we are here to experience unconditional love.

To Anne: Thank you for showing me how to get honest with myself.

To Katherine: Thank you for showing me how to give up my burdensome responsibilities and lighten up my life.

Inspiration

"I gave the best 20 years of my life to my family and it has taken them 20 years to recover from it."

My Mother: Elizabeth Yorgen

If I keep from meddling with people, they take
    care of themselves,
If I keep from commanding people, they behave
    themselves,
If I keep from preaching at people, they improve
    themselves,
If I keep from imposing on people, they become
    themselves.

                        The Way of Life, according to Lao-tzu

Contents

Acknowledgments

I gratefully acknowledge all of the many family members, friends, acquaintances and strangers I tried to rescue who refused to honor my wisdom, my insight, my help, even my good intentions. I am indebted as well to all of those people who tried in vain to give me the benefit of their experience and steer me in their right direction. Our mutual resistance to each other's truth reveals the secret to our recovery from rescuing. Each of us knows deep down in our heart exactly the path we need to walk for our own healing. The journey is simply lighter with a silent, supportive hand to hold.

With special thanks to Steve Taylor and Tracey Weingartner for pre-publication editorial assistance.

Preface

This book will be most helpful and healing for people who have defined their past in terms of co-dependency, dysfunctional family relationships, Adult Children of Alcoholics or Women Who Love Too Much. It is the next step for people who have acknowledged their "dis-ease" or their "addiction" and now just want to feel better.

If you have thought that you loved too much and are now withholding love from yourself and others, this material can help you be free to love again. If you have found that your growth in the self-help movement has further separated you from those you love, you will find communion here. If you have found it difficult to forgive your parents for their dis-ease, you will gain a new perspective. If you work with dysfunctional families, you will appreciate some refreshing ideas for spiritual and attitudinal healing.

With this book I invite you to remove the medical and psychological labels of your past perception as you would remove the training wheels from a bicycle. It is time to trust in the invisible power of spiritual order and balance . . . time to let go of "dis-ease" and enjoy a smoother, unencumbered ride towards a rich and joyful life.

Jackie Castine
Birmingham, Michigan

Introduction

My name is Jackie Castine and I have been talking to audiences in the midwest for several years about my personal recovery from rescuing. When I first began, I was not recovered myself and was there because I thought people needed to hear what I had to say. Now when I am chided about rescuing people from rescuing, I know that I speak for myself. My purpose is to share my truth, not to fix anyone's life. I enjoy making the emotional connections with an audience and hope you will feel the same sense of energetic intimacy through my writing.

A new last name found me in December of 1986 and I legally adopted it. This allows me to write about my family and protect their anonymity. I also wish to acknowledge my membership in several anonymous self-help groups without violating their traditions of anonymity.

Now let's talk about credentials. I want you to know what I am not. I am not a psychologist, a therapist or a social worker. I have a Bachelor of Arts Degree and worked as a teacher in the early 1970s before leaving the classroom for a 10-year career in corporate sales. My real education, like yours no doubt, came from my experience with life so I gave myself a new degree last year.

The H.B. Degree acknowledges that I am a Human Being engaged in an unlimited practice. Formerly I was a Human Doing engaged in playing God and rehearsing my role as a Messiah. During my recovery from rescuing I discovered a psychological and spiritual truth: that in acknowledging and accepting the limitations of our humanness, we transcend them.

I sometimes call myself a battle-scarred veteran of the rescuing war. For many years I thought I was fighting against an external enemy, chemical dependency, but as I tended to the wounded, I realized that the real battle was within myself . . . I was addicted to rescuing.

I am the adult child of an alcoholic. My father was a gregarious salesman whose drinking revolved around his work. We did not recognize that he had a drinking problem until his retirement when he bottomed out and went into treatment. I don't think we ever saw him drunk, but later I wondered how much we saw him sober.

You probably know that 50% of the time daughters of alcoholic fathers marry alcoholics. My twin sister and I were no exception. We unwittingly fulfilled any Mother's dream and our own psychological destiny. She married a doctor, I married a lawyer. We could not see that they had drinking problems. They looked pretty normal to us. She had no children. I have one son, 26, and two daughters who are now 21 and 23. Both my son and my oldest daughter are recovering alcoholics and have been in the AA 12-step recovery program for five years. I was divorced from my husband 14 years ago and he died five years ago from cancer of the liver at age 49.

My story is not unlike many divorced co-dependent adult children of alcoholics. I was an overachiever who was determined to be professionally successful in a nontraditional occupation. I exemplified the new liberated woman of the 70s, trying to balance family responsibilities with career plus some personal "time out for good behavior." Underneath the day-to-day stress I was operating with all the intact defense mechanisms of the co-dependent personality: controlling, low self-esteem, compulsive, denial of feelings, trouble with intimacy, perfectionism, people-pleasing, over-responsibility, substance abuse and work addiction. I was doing my strong woman number.

Like a circus performer balancing 10 plates on 10 poles and keeping them all spinning, I was a sight to behold. Superwoman in action! I was an account representative for a large corporation handling a two million dollar territory, had written a book on career change, ran a consulting business on the side, was present at school conferences and plays, maintained a relationship with a significant other, worked out at the health club, inquired after my mother's well-being and took pride in being in control of my life. My friends were breathless at my performance: some in awe and envy, some waiting for the plates to fall. I was too busy staying in action to feel anything.

If my life had the frenzied activity of a three-ring circus, there was a drama going on in one corner that ultimately made me take my focus off my balance and control act in the center ring. It wasn't long before everything came crashing down.

My son had been a problem child from the moment he was born. He came into the world kicking and screaming, angry, it seemed, for having been born. What was this inexplicable pain he felt, this innocent child? Helpless to ease his pain and fearful that I was causing it increased the tension. Irritability in infancy grew to aggression and hyperactivity in early childhood. With his two younger sisters to care for, a husband who was often away building his career, John's unpredictable behavior had me on the edge of what I feared the most . . . losing control.

I set out to find out what was wrong and got a diagnosis. Hyperkinetic Impulse Disorder the experts called it. I wonder to this day if I am the only mother who was happy to hear that her child had "brain damage." The label had a curious way of stilling the pangs of guilt I felt for having nurtured this condition. I preferred to believe that the randomness of nature was the villain. The experts recommended Ritalin, a structured environment and counseling . . . for *me*! I was ready to begin a long slow but steady path towards personal transformation.

Finding the answers to the question *why* does not always solve the problem and this was very clear to me as John grew up. If he was difficult to deal with when he was five, things were worse when he was 10. Despite medication for him, counseling for me, many different schools, many doctors, many forms of behavior modification, there were escalating behavioral problems in school, in the neighborhood and at home. Well-meaning but ill advised "constructive criticism" from family eroded my self-esteem and my ability to cope. His proneness to accidents caused me to fear for his safety and his unpredictable angry outbursts threatened me, my daughters and ultimately my marriage. Boarding school seemed the only way out. With guilt, grief and relief we sent John away from home.

The marriage dissolved anyway by mutual consent. Our son entered the turbulence of adolescence and with his predisposition to drug usage, he was soon unable to function in school. We tried to find a place where he could be contained. There were several public and private schools, the military system and Synanon. At 17 he could not function in a structure and was too young to be on his own but I had now become involved in a 12-step program and was getting ready to let go.

Two days before Christmas of 1980 I received a phone call in the middle of the night. Home on leave from the Navy, John had gone out drinking with some old friends. Awakened from a light sleep I heard his husky voice on the other end of the line. "Mom, something real bad has happened. I'm in jail. I stabbed somebody!"

It was the end of the line. The last straw. There would be no more tears for me. No more searching. No more things to do. No more efforts to make. I was finished. I surrendered to my own powerlessness. I knew in that moment that his tragedy was my salvation. An indescribable peacefulness came over me and I was free from the struggle of trying to save him. I look back on it now as a gift. I did not know it then, but the end was truly the beginning . . . the beginning of my recovery from rescuing.

1

Rescuing
Why Not?

What Is Rescuing?

Here's what the dictionary says:

Rescue: To free or deliver from confinement, violence, danger or evil. Syn. liberate, release, save, redeem, ransom, extricate.

Help: To contribute strength or means to, render assistance to, cooperate effectively with, to relieve someone in need, pain, sickness, distress. A means of remedying or stopping something. Furnishing anything that furthers another's efforts or relieves his wants or necessities.

What's Wrong With Rescuing?

There's nothing wrong with it if it works. If you feel good giving assistance and the other people find your assistance helpful, you have nothing to recover from.

This book is for people who have not been getting the results they were looking for from their helping behavior. Maybe
you found people didn't appreciate what you did for them.
Maybe you suspect you are helping too much. Maybe you
found that the down-on-their-luck ones just kept having more
bad luck. Maybe you found you were becoming resentful. Did
you begin to wish that someone would rescue you?

For the moment, set aside considerations of right or wrong
and ask yourself, "How does my rescuing or helping
behavior make me feel? How does it make the other person
feel? What result am I looking for? Do I want a change in
their behavior, attitude or lifestyle? A sense of peacefulness,
happiness and well-being for me and for them?"

*The question is not "Is helping right or wrong?" but "Does
it feel happy, harmonious and complete to both giver and
receiver?"*

Chances are if you picked up this book, rescuing and
helping, either practiced in your personal life or professionally in the service occupations, is making you uncomfortable.
You are already questioning your own attitudes, beliefs and
behavior because a relationship or your job is not working
for you.

Perhaps you based your life on service to others and now
find that the burden of caring for others is making you sick.
You can remember your compassion, your desire to make
the world a better place, the joy you received from feeling
that you make a difference in people's lives, the sense of
connection you used to get from nurturing relationships.

You may have found that your helping behavior is keeping
a loved one helpless. Perhaps you have a child or children
who don't want to grow up. You may wish to divorce yourself
from their problems and still hold onto a loving relationship
with them. Perhaps you have a spouse who is unable to
manage his part in family responsibilities. Perhaps you find
you are carrying his end as well as your own. Perhaps you
have noticed that you are being rejected by the very ones you
have been trying to help.

Maybe you are surrounded at home and at work by people
who depend on you more than you wish. Some of you may

have taken on the responsibilities of aging parents when your siblings cannot or choose not to be involved. You may be aware that you are in several of these roles simultaneously. Just as you get rid of one dependency problem, another crops up before you have a chance to catch your breath.

It takes two to play the rescuing game: the helper and the helpless, the alcoholic and the enabler, the dependent and the co-dependent, the doctor and the patient, the shoulder to lean on and the heavy depressed head. You may have found you've invited a bear to dance or accepted an invitation from the bear and now you can't sit down until the bear gets tired. What started out as fun has become exhausting.

How Can Rescuing Be An Addiction?

Since I discovered my destructive rescuing pattern in the context of chemical dependency, I like to talk about rescuing as an addiction. If we don't have a predisposition to addictive behavior, we can enjoy helping others on a selective basis, free to choose when it is convenient for us to do so. We don't have an attraction to it. We can control it. It doesn't control our lives.

Like a glass of wine before dinner or a casual beer at the ball game, helping someone just gives us a nice warm relaxed feeling about other people and life. We aren't uncomfortable if we abstain. We don't feel guilty if we say *NO*.

A rescuer on the other hand is a compulsive helper, someone who cannot keep from stepping in to give aid, even when it is unsolicited. I found that my behavior was the outer projection of my inner belief that there is a right way to live, a right way to do things. It was my way, of course, and I knew just what the other people should do to make their life better. It was my duty, obligation and responsibility to get them on the right path and keep them there at all costs. I was in the diagnose-and-treat business, whether I was in the role of wife, mother, teacher or consultant.

Like the alcoholic we begin to suspect that we have a problem if we see a repeating pattern in our lives: If we promised ourselves we would say no, and we were powerless to do it. I found that at one point in my life I was acting like a frustrated one-woman Coast Guard rescue squad . . . pulling one drowning victim after another out of hot water, getting them up on shore just to see them all jumping back in as soon as I had saved them.

If we see that our helping behavior is keeping a loved one helpless, or if we are uncomfortable and resentful because others don't take our advice or appreciate our efforts to help, we know we may be moving from constructive helping to addictive enabling.

Do You Recognize Your Pattern?

There are lots of little quizzes for drinkers to take to see if they have crossed the line from social drinking to alcohol abuse. Here's one for rescuers. Unlike those other tests this one has no score, no right or wrong answers, no pass or fail. The feeling you get from taking the test will give you the answer. You can even cheat a little and kid yourself if you want to. And then when you're ready to feel better, you can tell the truth and change your life.

The Rescuer's Quiz

1. Has the primary focus in your life been in serving the needs of others?

2. Are you in or drawn to one of the service professions: teaching, nursing, social work, the ministry?

3. Have there been addicted people in your family? Father? Mother?

4. Has your self-esteem been wrapped around your image of yourself as a super-mom or super-neighbor or the guy who's the last to leave the office at night?

5. Are you the first one through the door with a casserole when somebody dies?

6. Are you the oldest child in the family? Are you the one everyone depends on? The one who can always be counted on to do the job and do it right?

7. When you attend a lecture or a class, do you always think, "Oh, Mary should be here. She would really benefit from this." As you are reading this book, are you thinking about who else *needs* to read it?

8. Is it hard for you to take time for yourself and have fun?

9. Do you believe you are responsible for making other people happy?

10. Do you find yourself being resented when you were only trying to be helpful?

11. Do you find yourself giving advice that is not welcome or accepted?

12. Do you think you know what is best for other people?

13. Do you often feel that no matter how much you do, it isn't enough?

14. Has the former pleasure you used to get from loving and caring given way to feelings of exhaustion and resentment?

15. Are you especially critical of others who don't do their share?

If you found yourself feeling defensive about any of your answers, you will notice that you have placed yourself in a self-righteous position. You can only get out of your rescuing behavior when you stop making excuses for it.

For example, maybe you found yourself thinking, *"Of course, I can't relax and have any fun. My whole life has been tied up with taking care of Mother since my sister and her husband retired to play golf in Florida!"* You and I both know that as long as we justify our feelings of anger or resentment at being a victim of any situation, we are powerless to change it.

How Does This Happen To Nice People Like Us?

It wasn't difficult for most of us. In our western culture and Judeo-Christian tradition we were raised to believe that our purpose, even duty, in the world is to serve our fellow man. We understand the nature of mutual support systems. "No man is an island. No man stands alone." And we learned at an early age that we didn't want to stand alone either. We gave to others to get love and approval.

Maybe you, too, started out innocently, just enjoying the feeling of well-being we all get from being able to lend a helping hand. Of course, we liked the appreciation we received. Everyone told us how nice we were. We used to feel good when we helped someone. The feeling made us high. Now we are depressed. All we get is more trouble. The person we are rescuing isn't getting better or stronger. He or she appears to be getting worse. The person we love becomes a villain. Where love once existed, we now feel only bitterness and resentment. These loving connections are no longer making our life more pleasant but have become ties that bind too tightly.

You know you've crossed the line between social helping and compulsive obsessive enabling, when what used to make you feel good, now makes you feel bad.

When the same old stuff is producing a different result . . . it's time to stop "using!"

2

Helping
How Do I
Get Hooked?

How Can I Avoid The Compulsive Helping Cycle?

Look before you leap! Remember, your perception of their need is the thing that gets you hooked. Relationships based on need are usually destructive in some way. Let love be your only motive for helping, then there is no sense of giving and taking. When I am presented with a situation which appears to require my assistance or a request for help I ask myself, What are my needs? Do I want to do this? Why do I want to do it? How will I feel if I don't? What's the pay-off for me?

Do I Have A Hidden Agenda?

We must ask ourselves, what is my real motive in helping someone? Whose interest am I really serving? Is it true that all service is self-serving? Was my giving designed to get something in return? Is altruism a masquerade for approval-seeking or power plays? Does my low self-esteem urge me into a morally superior stance of helping? Can I create intimacy only with those who need me? And finally does my attention to others keep the focus off my own needs? Do I think I shouldn't have any?

How Do I Get Hooked?

I want to be thought of as a good person, a loving mother, a kind neighbor, a contributing member of the community. I want approval. I don't want anyone to accuse me of not doing my duty. I am afraid of criticism. I am afraid that if I don't do it, no one else will. I like the feeling of being needed.

I personally found that moral concern about the right thing to do was not particularly helpful. The "shoulds" kept piling up and created a great weight in my life.

I came to see that I had misunderstood God's plan for me. Some spiritual truths came out of the pain. First, I have nothing to give to others if I am not caring for myself. I must give to myself first. Second, I am vulnerable to manipulation by others only when I am not honest with myself about my motives for giving. They are not the villains. They are the divine instruments through which I discover my own integrity.

I clearly remember a small but significant experience with my daughter while she was away at college. I had driven up to see her with my mother and had looked forward to a nice long bath in the motel room after the four-hour drive but she wanted me to pick her up at the dorm right away to go shopping at K-Mart. I nobly gave up my desire to accommodate hers.

While we were pushing the cart around, she asked, "How come you're not being very nice to me?" I thought I was being "nice" by meeting her request and my mother expressed her dismay at my daughter's "ingratitude." Actually my daughter was giving me an opportunity to get honest. She picked up on the attitudinal truth behind the behavior and confronted me with my hypocrisy. She knew I really didn't want to be there. I knew that I had learned a valuable lesson in relationships.

Now I know that when I am present out of a sense of guilt, duty or obligation, I am participating in a business deal, not an act of generosity. There is nothing wrong with that arrangement, but I will not expect it to be an emotionally joyful experience.

How Can I Help Myself?

Perhaps your father is in a nursing home and you know he welcomes your visits. You feel sorry that you can't care for him in your own home. You wish he was in better health and would like to ease his loneliness. On the other hand you are already burdened with a full-time teaching job, husband, children and home which require your attention and your energy. You see and feel the trap but don't know how to manage it. The pattern for a rescuer would be to take control, be the strong one, set up a plan to fit it all in, to smile, to push yourself, to take the bows when everyone tells you how wonderfully self-sacrificing you are.

If this is your pattern . . . *STOP!* This is precisely the time to be a receiver. Ask for help and support from others. Let your 13-year-old learn how to cook. Hire someone to help with the housework. Start getting a weekly massage.

I listen to many men and women who attend my lectures and workshops. They are there because they want to change their pattern. They tell me they have focused on the needs of others for so many years, they do not have any idea what they want to do or even like to do.

How Can I Help Others?

Often letting go of the role of rescuer frees us to simply just love with empathy and understanding. A friend of mine spoke of the "Code Blue" phenomenon she has observed in her duties as a floor nurse in intensive care.

Sometimes after everything medically possible has been done to aid a dying patient, all support systems are withdrawn and a blue sign is hung over the bed. When the medical attention stops, the patient mysteriously and spontaneously usually gets better. This parallels my experience with detaching from my children's alcoholism.

While I was trying to get them well, nothing happened. When I gave up, they gave in. Perhaps one of the most helpful things we can do in the supportive process is to give up our assumption that everyone who is sick wants to be cured. And we need to accept and understand that healing can take place in the absence of a cure for the disease.

Helping is most effective when it empowers the other person to help himself. We frequently help others because we see them as helpless. It is no wonder then that they become angry instead of grateful. We are so often caught in the trap of our limited vision. We sincerely believe that if we don't step in and help, no one else will. When we believe we are the single resource, we are playing God.

Perhaps the most helpful way to support a person in trouble is to empower them to see themselves with new eyes, to show them the potential of their own inner resources, to ask them what they would like to do about their situation instead of giving them advice.

The following is borrowed from the literature of Families Anonymous, a self-help support group (see Appendix). You might wish to place a copy on your refrigerator as a daily reminder of your commitment to recover from rescuing.

Helping

My role as helper is not to do things for the person I am trying to help, but to *be* things; not to try to control and change his actions, but through understanding and awareness, to change my reactions. I will change my negatives to positives, fear to faith, contempt for what he does to respect for the potential within him, hostility to understanding and manipulation or overprotectiveness to release with love, not trying to make him fit a standard or image, but giving him an opportunity to pursue his own destiny, regardless of what his choice may be. I will change my dominance to encouragement, panic to serenity, the inertia of despair to the energy of my own personal growth and self-justification to self-understanding.

Self-pity blocks effective action. The more I indulge in it, the more I feel that the answer to my problems is a change in others and in society, not in myself. Thus I become a hopeless case.

Exhaustion is the result when I use my energy in mulling over the past with regret, or in trying to figure ways to escape a future that has yet to arrive. Projecting an image of the future and anxiously hovering over it for fear that it will or it won't come true, uses all my energy and leaves me unable to live today. Yet living today is the only way to have a life.

I will have no thought for the future actions of others, neither expecting them to be better or worse as time goes on, for in such expectations I am really trying to create. I will love and let be.

All people are always changing. If I try to judge them, I do so only on what I think I know of them, failing to realize that there is much I do not know. I will give others credit for attempts at progress and for having had many victories which are unknown.

I, **too am always changing**, and I can make that change a constructive one, if I am willing. *I can change myself.* Others I can only love.

3

Responsibility
What Am I
Responsible For?

What Is My Responsibility?

"Mothers take care of their children."
"It's a father's duty to provide for his family."
"Honor thy father and thy mother."
"I am responsible for my wife's or husband's happiness."

These beliefs are traditional mandates that have supported the family system for many centuries. Agricultural societies, which were characterized by an extended family support system, have given way to the impersonal and isolated lifestyle of an urban culture. We have seen the breakdown of family as a result. Modern technology has freed most of us from the bare survival level and has given us time to think about life, liberty and the pursuit of individual happiness. Times have changed for better or for worse. Most of us have faced the conflict of: Who am I responsible to? What am I responsible for? Where does my responsibility to others end? Where does my responsibility to myself begin?

I found myself questioning my maternal role when my best efforts could not keep my accident-prone son safe and secure. It haunted me later as his aggressive, violent behavior at home threatened his sisters' mental and physical health. What conflicts arise when men lose their jobs or find that they are physically killing themselves to put the children through college? What do we do when Mom wants to come and live with us and our loyal hard-working husband is ready to retire and travel the country in a motor home?

The word "responsibility" is tightly intertwined with guilt for many of us. We remember the disapproving parent standing over the broken cookie jar saying, "Who's responsible for this?" I found it helpful to redefine responsibility as "the ability to respond" to clear the conscience and clarify the situation.

The ability to respond means taking total responsibility for the situation. As difficult as this is when you are in a crisis, it is the most powerful mind-altering idea you can ingest. Now my responsibility becomes the willingness to see that the conflict I have about a situation is self-created because of the way I see it. Instead of trying to manipulate other people or outer circumstances, I become ready to change my perception. I have discovered that when I change my perception of the situation, the pain of the conflict goes away.

I have learned that my self-created conflicts are always purposeful. They exist so that I can learn about myself and the life experience. When I take the responsibility for creating my own pain, I discover that I can create my freedom from it. The depressing alternative is to believe that I am a victim of circumstances and that I am powerless. In the past I believed that this was true for myself and for other people. It was precisely that belief that kept me trying to rescue others from their self-inflicted pain.

I am well aware that at first glance it seems that I am abdicating empathy, caring, doing for others, to pursue a selfish approach to life. Actually I have found that fearless and honest self-examination allows me to be more, not less, responsive to other people.

How Do We Learn To Take The Responsibility For Ourselves?

1. Give up our victim pose. We will never again blame anyone else for anything we do or don't do, any condition we have or don't have, any emotion that hurts. I know that the only way out of my victim position is to "own my own stuff." Eleanor Roosevelt said, "No one can offend me without my permission." Remind yourself that there are no victims, only volunteers.

2. Responsibility means I won't blame myself. I will not make myself the villain or the victim. It means I will be acutely aware of what is going on, see my part in it, especially the pay-offs I get from my suffering. I will practice not judging myself for creating the problem.

3. I will stop spending my life reacting to situations and I will take charge of my life. Now I can convert the energy I had previously spent trying to control others into re-creation for myself. I dance to a new tune which I learned from Arnold Patent's book *You Can Have It All*. He calls it **The Three Step Dance of Life**.

   a) Look what I created!
   b) I will not judge it right or wrong.
   c) How would I rather feel instead?

   When we first learn the steps, we spend more time on the first two beats and sometimes never get to the last one. The dance champs learn the rhythm that takes them quickly over the problem and the nonjudgment into the light-hearted creative movement towards solution.

When Is It Time To Re-create Your Re-sponsibilities?

1. When you have a lot of irresponsible people around you, you need to recognize that you attract them. Can't you see that you are wearing a neon sign on your

forehead saying, "Do you need someone to take care of
you? Let me volunteer for the job." Have you noticed
how often you get rid of one and another comes in to
fill the empty space?

2. When you find yourself being judgmental or critical of
   others who don't meet their responsibilities according
   to your definition, keep in mind that the behavior or
   attitudes we find most annoying in others is a mirror to
   our own internal conflict.

3. When you feel resentment because you have taken on
   the responsibilities of someone else, you think you are
   resentful because they aren't doing their share, but you
   are really angry at yourself because you couldn't say no.

What Is Over-responsibility?

One of the patterns I noticed in myself and other Adult
Children of Alcoholics was the issue of over-responsibility. I
learned that I have a tendency to play God. I want to be
omniscient and omnipotent. I really believe that if it had
been in my power to make the sun rise and set every day, I
would have been delighted to have the job. Lord knows, I
took on all kinds of other controlling activities that were not
in my sphere of influence. And over-responsibility is
addictive because there are so many rewards for it at home
and at work. After all CEOs, surgeons and Mother Theresa
probably all have this condition. There is nothing wrong with
taking on the weight of the world unless the burden
immobilizes you. Those of us with the rescuing addiction
must really ask ourselves constantly, "Whose job is this? Do I
really want to do it?"

How Does Letting Go Of Responsibility Help Others?

By adopting a model of 100% responsibility for all of our
actions, thoughts and feelings, we become a living model for
our children. We are no longer caught in the trap of
manipulation by guilt. We see that it is our duty and
obligation to allow our loved ones the freedom to choose
how they wish to live and perhaps even how and when they

wish to die. We grant them the freedom to experience the consequences of the decisions they make. We know that we learn from cause and effect. There are no failures, only results or lack of results. We recognize that all discomfort is precisely what leads people into new ways of doing and being.

We often find that when we give up "shoulding on ourselves," we respond to the needs of others by choice, not from an unexamined hidden agenda of duty and obligation. When we operate from freedom, not fear, we find a much wider range of options available to us.

For example, I noticed that I was upset with my daughter's financial problems. I offered her the benefit of my experience because I thought it was my duty as her mother to do so. I noticed that I didn't get the desired result. She didn't take my advice and resented my interference. I kept doing it until I was willing to get honest about my real issue. I had a hidden agenda. I secretly felt that if I had been a good mother, I would have trained her properly to pay her bills and she wouldn't be in this situation. In feeling that I was responsible for her irresponsibility, I then thought I "should" volunteer the money. Perhaps you have done that, too? Perhaps, like me, you even did it more than once. In this situation my heightened sense of responsibility was a mask for guilt.

Maybe you have found yourself picking up the pieces of other people's bad decisions so they didn't have to feel the pain. Maybe it is our own pain we are really trying to alleviate. If this is a pattern for you, you must deal with it or it will escalate. I believe that we continue to create the same conflicted situations until we learn the lessons they present. It is not at all uncommon in my support group to find a family member has given up rescuing the child they thought was helpless and irresponsible only to find that a year later, there was a baby on the scene who needed rescuing from an alcoholic child who had become a parent. It is not wrong to interfere or right to let go. Each situation is unique. Our ability to respond with happy results for all is enhanced by our willingness to be aware of the whole picture . . . our patterns, our guilt, our perception of responsibility.

If I Give Up My Old Ideas About Duty, Obligation And Responsibility, What Will Replace It?

The following material is a 9-Step Program for Change. It was written by Jud Decker and Arnold Patent, both of whom demonstrate personal commitment to these principles in their lives. I am grateful to them for their teaching by example. You might want to use these steps as a daily meditation or as a support group structure.

Commitment To Life

1. **Trust**

    I know that my Higher Power/Perfection/Infinite Intelligence/God Within is my true source of peace, harmony and abundance.

2. **Free Will**

    I finally accept that I am responsible for my life and that everything that happens to me I create consciously or unconsciously.

3. **Nonjudgment**

    I have made a decision not to judge anything or anybody including myself.

4. **Forgiveness**

    I choose to practice forgiving everyone for whom I feel less than unconditional love.

5. **Oneness**

    I choose to practice seeing the perfection in everyone just the way they are.

6. **Love**

    I recognize that fear is withholding love so I choose to practice feeling unconditional love for those people, places and things whenever I experience fear.

7. **Joy**

    I accept that any improvement in the quality of my life is my own responsibility, so I choose to feel the joy within me more and more each day.

8. **Gratitude**

I realize that the universe is a mutual support system so I choose to use every situation as an opportunity to gratefully give and receive support.

9. **Purpose**

Finally, I commit to regularly reviewing and upgrading my life's purpose, seeking greater understanding of God's will for me and the power to carry that out.

A sign I noticed last week on a church bulletin board:

"Freedom and responsibility are twins, not enemies."

4

Detachment
How Can I Let Go?

The following is a reprint of a flyer which has been circulating around 12-Step groups of Al-Anon and Families Anonymous for quite some time. It describes better than I can what it means to "let go."

Let Go . . .

To *"let go"* does not mean to stop caring, it means I can't do it for someone else.

To *"let go"* is not to cut myself off, it's the realization I can't control another.

To *"let go"* is not to enable, but to allow learning from natural consequences.

To *"let go"* is to admit powerlessness, which means the outcome is not in my hands.

To *"let go"* is not to try to change or blame another, it's to make the most of myself.

To *"let go"* is not to care for, but to care about.

To *"let go"* is not to fix, but to be supportive.

To *"let go"* is not to judge, but to allow another to be a human being.

To *"let go"* is not to be in the middle arranging all the outcomes, but to allow others to affect their destinies.

To *"let go"* is not to be protective, it's to permit another to face reality.

To *"let go"* is not to deny, but to accept.

To *"let go"* is not to nag, scold or argue, but instead to search out my own shortcomings and correct them.

To *"let go"* is not to adjust everything to my desires, but to take each day as it comes and cherish myself in it.

To *"let go"* is not to criticize and regulate anybody, but to try and become what I dream I can be.

To *"let go"* is not to regret the past, but to grow and live for the future.

To *"let go"* is to fear less and love more.

Anonymous

How Can I Possibly Do This?

You can't force yourself to let go. It is not a will-power issue. This is a release process. We release our resistance. You can observe yourself and others holding on. You can love yourself through the discomfort. You can gently remind yourself to ask for help from a power greater than yourself. You can be patient with yourself for being afraid to let go. And one day when you least expect it . . . you receive the gift of surrender.

1. Open yourself up to the idea.
2. Observe without judgment how your attempts to control, to arrange outcomes have failed.
3. Become aware of the feeling in your body when you are frustrated by the energy spent trying to make things happen or prevent things from happening.

4. Start small. Don't ask, "Where are you going?" "Don't forget to . . ." Then build up to the more difficult things, such as letting the person cover their own debts, etc.

5. Notice how things resolve themselves without your interference.

A first-hand account from a recovering rescuer: "There is such a feeling of elation in me when I watch myself not getting involved in the problem. I'm like a little kid who's just learning to ride a bike. It's a wonderful new free feeling but I know I'm not ready to go 'no hands' yet!"

6. When you have changed the pattern just a little, you have a stronger resistance to being pulled back into the rescuing game. You have some positive experiences behind you and will be less vulnerable to manipulation.

7. You will notice how when you pull out of the rescuing game, someone else appears to play the rescuer. You will be tempted to play rescuer to this other person who is being drawn in. Avoid doing this. People need to learn from their own experience. You may observe that the other family members are emotionally upset. It is a good reinforcement for you to see in others' behavior that you once acted out. Be a model of detachment by not reacting.

8. Eventually when all of the enablers in the family have tried and tired out their rescuing wings, the dependent person gets himself out of the trouble. He takes on his own stuff when he can't find anyone else to do it. This is the ultimate recovery towards responsibility for the whole family. It takes time. Be patient.

Don't be discouraged if you relapse. It's helpful for all of us, drug dependent and co-dependent, to view relapse not as failure but simply as a progressive step towards real long-lasting freedom from addiction. Detachment with love came after I had experienced detachment with anger and detachment with apathy. Ask yourself, "Have I really bottomed out?"

For me, this meant trying 28 ways to help and trying them all at least twice. For you, it may be more or less. Most controlling personalities have to be pretty exhausted before we surrender.

Ed F. said, "I only let go when I was too tired to hang on any longer."

Blanche D. told me, "I never let go of anything that didn't have claw marks all over it."

Betty H. testifies, "We reached the end of the line. We knew our emotional survival depended on it. We could honestly say we had done everything."

Belief in a Higher Power helps in the detachment process. The 12-Step program says we "came to believe." It is said (1) we came, (2) we came to and (3) we came to believe. That is to say we attended meetings, we woke up and our intellectual skepticism was transformed into faith in something outside of ourselves. For me, the "It," the random hostile universe, became a "Thou." And I believe it is always a purposeful and consistent teacher. And when I believe in accidents, I deny myself the opportunity to learn the lesson which has been presented. The infinite intelligence of my understanding does not conform to my petitions but rather is always showing me and my loved ones through the laws of synchronicity how we can conform to its harmony.

Your higher power can be God, Infinite Intelligence, the power of the Universe, the power of the 12 steps, the support group or love. If we believe we are releasing our loved ones to a hostile universe, letting go means abandoning them to death or chaos. We then feel we are pushing them out or cutting them off. This tough love approach carries with it all of the pain we would have if we chopped off our own right arm!

Detachment is a positive practice based on the quiet assurance that comes with the development of spiritual trust. I have known many atheists and agnostics who came to believe in a power greater than themselves precisely as a result of finding out they couldn't do it for another person.

Many who come into recovery from rescuing are from traditional religious backgrounds. They became disillusioned because prayer did not work. We wanted what we wanted for our loved ones.

"God helps those who help themselves" becomes "God helps those who let Him do his job." We can stop playing God ourselves. We can stop telling God what he should do and adopt the serenity prayer.

God grant me the serenity to accept the things I cannot change, the courage to change the things I can and the wisdom to know the difference.

I believe these concepts are best put into practice with the help of a support system, be it a 12-Step program, a universal principles network, a master-mind partnership or a church. When our lives have been predicated on being the strong ones, going it alone and doing for others, we benefit from placing ourselves in an environment where we can receive love and acceptance.

Guilt
Where Would We Be Without Guilt?

Columnist Erma Bombeck said, "Guilt is the gift that keeps on giving."

Bob Mandel wrote in *Open Heart Therapy* (Celestial Arts: Berkeley, California):

"Guilt is the Mafia of the mind. It is a protection plan we sell ourselves in order to avoid anticipated punishment. The only problem is that this particular form of protection involves self-punishment. All guilt is masochistic. The thought is 'If only I suffer enough, I'll be forgiven! If only I punish myself enough, maybe people will take pity on me and not hurt me!' Guilt is based on the illusion that pain is redemption rather than innocence. Guilt makes martyrs think they are saints. Guilt is the godfather masquerading as God . . . Guilt is not content until you make the supreme sacrifice of your life. In your death your ego laughs and dances on your grave. Guilt is hereditary. At every birth the torch is passed on . . . The antidote is to see that we create our own pain and pleasure as do others. Forgiveness frees us from guilt. *We must first forgive ourselves for pretending to be guilty.*"

For most of us that is a pretty tall order. We have been convinced that guilt serves us as purposefully as pain. We believe we need it to be self-correcting. We need to be whipped in order to stay in line. If we no longer fear the wrath of any angry fundamentalist God on Judgment Day what will happen to the human race?

I stopped feeling guilty for what I had done and what I hadn't done when I could see that holding on to it didn't move me along to another place. My experience was that the guilt immobilized me, rather than helped me change my situation.

What Is Conscience And How Is It Different From Guilt?

Bob Mandel makes an interesting and heartfelt distinction between guilt and conscience.

"Isn't guilt always self-disapproving? Isn't it the voice of fear? It seems to me that guilt is a voice in our head from the past, which is an illusion. What is the conscience but another voice? Conscience speaks to us in the present. It is the voice of the heart reminding us of what we really value. It tells us that our truth is that we have the potential to be unconditionally loving. It tells us we can trust our intuition, It tells us that even our guilt and suffering were based on love. It moves us to act out of love for ourselves and others."

I think this idea parallels the awareness we feel of a spiritual presence within us as opposed to the rules and commandments imposed by an external intellectual concept of God.

How Can I Begin To See A No-Fault Universe?

Here is an exercise from *Open Heart Therapy* that can help you see how the cycle of guilt and pain is self-created.

Make a list of 10 things you think you've done to hurt others.

(I wrote on my list that I didn't listen to my children when they needed me. I identified being unable to feel and express love for family members. I sent my son to military school when he was only nine years old and I physically punished him when I was out of control with my anger.)

1. _____
2. _____
3. _____
4. _____
5. _____
6. _____
7. _____
8. _____
9. _____
10. _____

Make a second list of 10 things you think others have done to hurt you.

(I knew I had been hurt by my husband's infidelities, my son's stealing from me to get money for drugs, my mother's need to control and her fear of feelings. And finally, my father's emotional and frequent physical absence.)

1. _____
2. _____
3. _____
4. _____
5. _____
6. _____
7. _____
8. _____
9. _____
10. _____

Take a long look at both lists. Realize that your guilt feelings cause you to seek punishment. Others will accommodate your subconscious request for punishment by hurting you. Forgive and accept yourself and others will no longer hurt you.

Further, Mandel writes:

"Simply become aware that no one is ever at fault; that guilt and punishment are always seeking each other out, pattern attracting pattern, victim and victimizer in unspoken agreement."

This can be a powerfully intuitive exercise in forgiveness as well.

Recently in a support group I heard a woman speak for the first time of how her older brother had intimidated her into sex play when she was eight and how frightened, ashamed and angry she felt for so many years. She could not forgive him for doing it, herself for going along with it or her mother for not protecting her from it. The memory was keeping her from healthy dating relationships and the resentment caused discord in the family. We listened to her express the pain of her long held silent guilt, fear and shame. In the attentive and nonjudgmental atmosphere she saw the release of "confession" and shifted from the subject of being a victim to an incident which occurred when she was 13.

She was with her young friends who decided to play a prank on a blind old man in the neighborhood. They entered his house, did no physical damage, but frightened and terrorized him, then left. This story was revealed in a juxtaposition that allowed her to see her own shadow . . . to acknowledge her role as both victim and victimizer. Looking into her own mirror of anguish, she completed the cycle of awareness and saw her brother in both roles as well. She forgave everyone including herself. She was free from the past.

Fear ·
What Can I Do
When I'm Afraid
He Will Die?

What Is It?

*F*alse *E*vidence *A*ppearing *R*eal

Fear is false evidence appearing real? Nonsense, you say. "Even paranoids have real fears." Most of us believe that fear is real . . . that fear is what keeps us alive. But now we know that the adaptive diseases of the Twentieth Century are caused by the archaic biological response to fear.

The Flight or Fight Response which kept our primitive ancestors alive doesn't work for us. We are rarely faced with real lions but our minds and bodies still "act as if." It is emotional stress we face. Increased adrenalin with no place to go is killing us. Changing our perception is the only solution. We must begin to see that our lions are really pussycats.

Some of us fly in airplanes often and comfortably. Some of us fly with white knuckles. Some of us will never get in an airplane. The difference is in the way we think about it. Imagine yourself walking across a board lying flat on the ground in your backyard. It is 3 feet wide and 20 feet long. An easy stroll, right? Now imagine that the same board is 20 feet off the ground. This time it's not such an easy stroll. Same task, different perception.

Many of us have overcome situations that used to paralyze us. What happened to my fear of driving on the freeway? What happened to your fear of skiing as you now enjoy the thrill of descending the slopes? Did it magically disappear? Did you fight it? Lean into it? Feel it and do it anyway?

What Are We Afraid Of?

Rescuers in their typical "strong one" role are afraid to confront their fears. We fear death, our own and others. We fear pain, our own and others. Co-dependents fear dependency. Controllers fear being out of control. We fear there is something wrong with us. We fear we are at fault. We fear criticism. We fear abandonment. We are so afraid of dying that we are not able to really live.

How Can I Stop Rescuing When My Biggest Fear Is That She Will Die?

During the last 10 years I talked intimately with hundreds of parents who were concerned about their children's drug and alcohol abuse. They focused on poor grades, surly attitudes, poor money management and family disruptions. What they couldn't talk about was as obvious as the elephant in the living room: the fear that their child might die and they would feel responsible.

I was unable to break my enabling pattern until I acknowledged that my son might die. When I stopped the denial and confronted my own fear, head on, I was no longer manipulated by it. Our support groups can teach us to chant "I didn't cause it. I can't cure it." But when faced with the perception of a life-and-death situation, our emotional involvement keeps us rescuing. Was it Freud who told us that our deepest fear is a mirror to our darkest desire? If honesty eases our suffering, many of us might be willing to admit that we would be relieved if the alcoholic died, especially if we could go on with our lives guilt free.

How Can I Be Free From This Fear?

Most phobia clinics teach people how to live more comfortably with their fears, not eliminate them entirely. So how can you get to the place where you are no longer immobilized by the fear your child will die? Start by acknowledging it to yourself first and then to the one you fear for . . It can be a simple, nonaccusatory, nonmanipulative statement of caring and concern. When you can do this, you will find you have created a much wider range of options in the relationship. By revealing your fear you act as a model of personal integrity to someone who is keeping himself in bondage by his own secrets.

How Do I Handle A Suicide Threat?

While we need to take suicide threats seriously, we must also be acutely aware that they are often used as a manipulative tool by the chemically dependent person to keep parents and therapists locked into taking responsibility for the dependent's dis-ease.

By openly acknowledging suicide potential, you diffuse it as a manipulative technique and demonstrate the courage to investigate its gravity and intention. The message is "It's OK to talk about suicidal feelings." And again it is an opportunity to deliver the one message that can heal, "I love you."

"You know how much we care about you. You appear very depressed about your life. Have you been thinking about suicide? Some people consider it when life becomes too painful. I want you to know there is help available to you if you want it."

Let the person be responsible for the decision. It was helpful for me to change the perception that I must save someone from themselves. Instead I came to believe that if anyone is really intent on dying, I can't save her. I'm not that powerful. I can only love her. And that is the only healing power I have.

How Can I Help?

When my daughter was in her junior year of college, she went through a very confusing time. She was overloaded with work, confused about her future, unhappy in love and experiencing fear in taking a math equivalency exam. She went to a mental health clinic. She called me to say she was having a nervous breakdown and wanted to drop out of school. She told me that the counselor had told her depression was a result of being raised in a dysfunctional family. She said if life was going to be this painful, she didn't think she wanted to continue living it.

I had a choice of perceptions. I could see her condition as a cop-out, just a way to get out of a tough situation. I could view her as clinically depressed, a very "sick" suicidal case. I could see it as a transitional stage of developmental growing pains. I wondered if she had some unfinished dependency business with me before she could move on to her adult independence. I knew that my perception would probably guide me to the professional who would reinforce my preconceived belief.

Because I was recovered from rescuing, I decided to let her handle her own diagnosis and course of treatment. Because I was recovered from guilt and fear, I was not defensive about my role in her current problems. I knew I was innocent and responsible. I strongly believed that if I treated her as sick, she would see herself that way. I knew she was asking me for help. And I wanted to empower her to help herself towards a healthy responsible life.

She came home. I asked her what she needed. Hospitalized psychiatric treatment? Out-patient therapy with a counselor? A rest? Or a change of activity? When I confronted the suicide issue directly, she immediately reassured me that she wasn't interested. Detached from the emotional drama, but not indifferent to her pain, I could simply be with her in a troubled time. She decided she wanted to be relieved of the pressure of school and decided to get a job, see a counselor and asked me to participate in that process. I agreed and also let her pay for the part of her therapy which was not covered by my insurance. In three months she decided that living at home and working was not what she wanted, and she went back to school in the spring quarter.

My method of handling a crisis is not a prescription for anyone else. It is just one testimonial to healing power of freedom from guilt and fear.

What Else Are We Afraid Of?

We fear criticism. Co-dependents carry the burden of perfectionism. We like to think we're just pursuing excellence, but I think it's a cover-up. I found out just how much time and energy I spent . . . doing and not doing . . . to avoid criticism. I suspect that next to public speaking, fear of criticism may be right up there on the list.

We want successful children, not so much for their happiness but so they will reflect our parenting skills. We want the approval of our own parents. We are model employees. We handle the details. Come early and stay late. And we certainly wouldn't want anyone to accuse us of being selfish. Be everything to everybody is our motto.

We are always looking to see what *they* want before we know how to be with them. I do not have to tell you how much energy it takes to second guess the world. It certainly keeps us from finding out what we want. And who we really are.

Are Rescuers Afraid Of Life?

Yes!! I think our preoccupation with the impending death of others is a mirror to our fear that we are not really living.

"You know you are an addicted rescuer when you see that you are drowning and someone else's life flashes in front of your eyes!"

Blanche D.

7

Love

Is It Possible
To Love Too Much?

What Is Love?

Love: (1) A profoundly tender, passionate affection for a person of the opposite sex. (2) A feeling of warm personal attachment or deep affection as for a parent, child or friend. (3) Affectionate concern for the well-being of others. (4) Deep and enduring emotional regard. (5) The charity of the creator, reverence towards God . . .

Random House Dictionary

"Love is letting go of fear."

Gerald J. Jampolsky, M.D.

"Love is the will to extend one's self for the purpose of nurturing one's own or another's spiritual growth."

M. Scott Peck, M.D.

"Our essence is love and is always present. Beneath the overlays of doubts, fears and other emotions, we shall always find the real self. Any time we look for it in ourselves or others, it will be there."

Arnold M. Patent

"My love life is finally so wonderful that I'm ready for someone else to join me in it."

Jeff Cavanagh

As human beings we experience love in many forms. Sometimes anger is the closest we can come to expressing love. I remember that my dad always got mad when my sister and I were little and we got sick. It may be a distortion but it is love nonetheless.

As I notice the experiences I have with the emotions I identify with love, I need to remind myself that one form of love is not better than another but they feel differently. Love is never wrong.

I recently heard Unity Minister Karen Boland give a lesson on Love at the Church of Today in Warren, Michigan. She spoke to the audience about the difference between Agape and Eros as two forms of expressing love.

"**Eros** is the love that arises out of our needs. It is the part of us that looks for love on the outside. It is self-centered. It is self-suffering. It believes that there is not enough love to go around. It fears that love will go away. It holds on. It is jealous. It is manipulative. It is judgmental and self-critical. It is the love that turns itself on and off."

Karen Boland went on to describe what the Greeks referred to as a "higher form."

"**Agape** is divine love expressing through us. It is a love current that flows through us unceasingly. It is the inner light, electricity from God who uses us as His love conduit. It is universal and impersonal like the sun. It recognizes oneness. It loves without discrimination, without judgment. Like the sun it is always there in us but we must move away the clouds of our limited vision, our intellectual human nature, our doubt and our fear in order for it to shine in us. We must give it permission to shine. We must recognize its power and make a conscious decision to let it come through."

Her words rang very true for me. It seemed to me that all of the trouble that I had in my life was created to help me understand the difference between my human self with its addiction to love and my higher self with its desire to be reconnected to its divine source. I believe that all of your trouble . . . resentment against parents, anger at spouses, disappointment with children, impatience with clients . . . exists to teach you just one thing, *how to love yourself and others unconditionally.*

. Each relationship problem, each dis-ease, each unlovable person is a carefully designed lesson plan to teach us that we can transcend our misconceptions about love. We learn slowly and require many painful lessons but the Universe is patient. It brings us all eventually to an awareness of our spiritual nature. We erotic acorns have the capacity to grow into agape oaks.

What Is Tough Love?

For many years I practiced generic tough love. The emphasis was on the tough, not on the love. It wasn't wrong to do that. It just didn't work. It didn't give me the results I wanted. I learned from the experience that I was engaged in a power play with my children when I was exercising tough love. I learned that to surrender my position of parental authority I did not need to play doormat and put up with unacceptable behavior. I learned that what masquerades as a discipline or drug problem is a spiritual issue. The teenage rebellion caused me to confront my feelings of being out of control and my willful ego. On bringing these shadows to the light, "tough" turned into a quiet inner strength that is the basis for authority that no one questions.

My friend Claire from my 12-Step group wrote the following:

"I used to think if I practiced tough love it would be tough on my son. I found out it is tough on me. Tough love means I confront myself. I become willing to give up my old ideas about what love is. Years ago I shared my bitterness over my son's unacceptable behavior with a therapist. I told him of the grief I felt over the lost love. He confirmed my belief that relationships were based on reciprosity and that it was this exchange that nurtured love. This left me with no way to love my child.

"I was propelled by the pain of resentment, fear and diminished love toward the possibilities of practicing unconditional love. To me unconditional love means loving someone because he is a human being, deserving of dignity, respect and love, no matter what choices he has made in his life.

"The tough in tough love requires me to humble myself and recognize my powerlessness over another person's life. It means surrendering my position as benefactor, protector, manager, fixer-upper or the illusion of those roles. I am no longer the good guy sporting a white hat but I'm not the bad guy either. I'm not drawing my guns anymore and someday the holster is going to fall right off my hips."

Isn't It Possible To Love Too Much?

The problem isn't that we love them too much but that we didn't love ourselves enough. By confronting the illusion that love is a limited commodity, we begin to see that loving ourselves is loving others, and withholding from ourselves is withholding from others. Love is everywhere but we can't see it. We resist it, keep it away. We have been confused about self-love. Our belief has been, "Either I love myself or I love others" and "It is more blessed to give than to receive." When we are in our body, we are fooled by the illusion that we are separate. We are here to remember what we have forgotten. We are one.

8

Recovering
How And When?

I have watched the events of my life from a variety of perspectives. When I was a young woman in my 20s raising a family, I was not long out of college where I had been trained to take a scientific approach. *If they are sick, get treatment for them.* It was a very practical medical model based on objective reality.

In my 30s I had accumulated a parade of people, all of whom seemed to have problems. The more I got involved with the medical model, the more sick people I saw. The concept of alcoholism as a family disease got me into therapy where we focused on the psychology of the dysfunctional family. From this place I was looking at what happened, why it happened and how I could handle it better. The psychological model was interesting, albeit time-consuming, but the problem of the problem-people not getting fixed was the same.

I found out the reason *why* in the medical and psychological models but I had not found any peace of mind. So now

I was ready to try something else. I was introduced to 12-Step support groups in 1976. The self-help support groups I joined were for families of people who are chemically dependent and have behavioral problems. They use the same 12 suggested steps of Alcoholics Anonymous in their recovery programs. I was ready to surrender my highly prized intellect to a spiritual approach. Here are three windows for viewing the parade of life problems and problem people. Which vantage point have you experienced? Which makes the most sense to you?

Window 1: The Medical Model
Diagnose And Treat

When I was looking at my parade of problems from the basic street level of medical objectivity I was very close to the action. I was involved in the immediacy, the noise and the drama. I got caught up in playing doctor so that *they* could become "adjusted." Did you also read books to learn about their condition? Label them alcoholic, schizophrenic, neurotic, hyperkinetic, sociopathic or gifted? Did you, like me, line up medical experts to agree with in your diagnosis? Do you remember when your focus was on "curing the disease?"

For 15 years I was fully and actively engaged in trying to fix other people. I spent most of my time and energy focused on others' symptoms, shortcomings, attitudes and behavior. I was attentive to what they were doing and what was wrong with them. The game was diagnose and treat — and then repeat. I got high on information, accumulated statistics, spent hours on the phone, kept a file of agencies, took the sick ones around to doctors or spent my energy trying to convince them to go. "They" didn't improve. The more information I got, the worse I felt.

During this time I learned about chemical dependency as a disease. It was, and is, a helpful perspective because it moves us away from the window that labels the alcoholic as a weak person or a moral degenerate. This view helps us detach from the emotional and personal involvement with the unacceptable behavior of the person. We now define the disease as the villain. Some of us, however, found the view from this window paradoxical. We understood that they couldn't help it . . . that they were powerless over drugs and alcohol and yet we knew that they made a conscious decision to take the first and last pill, drink or fix. We also knew that their recovery would ultimately happen only when they made a *conscious decision to change.* And no one could do it for them. We began to see our own powerlessness in trying to fix the other person and we began to concentrate on our own addiction. We accepted that we were powerless over other people's lives and that the only person we could change was ourselves. When we made a conscious decision to do that, we gained a new perspective.

Window 2: The Psychological Model
Handle The Situation

This is a mezzanine view of the problem parade . . . a broader scope. Here we shift our focus from the other person's "illness" and attend to our ability to cope with the situation. At this stage I went into therapy for myself, accumulated a library on behavioral psychology and chemical dependency. I joined a support group. I still saw the problem people in my life as sick but now I saw myself as sick too. I was still interested in "the disease" . . . but this time it was my enabling addiction I was working on. I was feeling better because I was involved with people who had similar problems, people who understood.

But there were some new areas of discomfort for me. I noticed that what I focused on expanded. I saw addiction everywhere. Enablers behind every tree. Alcoholics hanging from the branches. All this awareness didn't seem to be contributing to my serenity. Where I had previously been obsessed with fixing my father, my husband, my son, now I was obsessed with fixing myself.

Maybe you've noticed or experienced that kind of frenetic activity that takes people in the transformational process from one theory, from one guru, from one seminar to another. The process is itself an addiction, occupying our hearts, our minds and our time. It is rooted in the belief that we are in pain because there is something basically wrong with us, and we are impatient to get it fixed. We want to learn to do it right. If I gave up trying to change the other person, now I have the red pencil out on myself. I am taking inventory, monitoring my actions and reactions. How am I doing? I have turned my judgment that others weren't living right to a judgment that I also need to learn the right way to cope with life.

Armed with a little knowledge, a misunderstanding of Step 12 and not recovered from rescuing, I found myself on a self-righteous crusade. I confronted two friends who were having drinking problems. At the time I thought I was acting out of love, concern and knowledge about the disease. I thought I could help them. You can guess that they were not at all receptive to me, my opinion or my knowledge.

Once again I experienced the symptoms of my rescuing compulsion. From a disease perspective I thought I was looking at their resistance and denial. I could not see that I was just choosing to be right rather than peaceful. So I was uncomfortable again. The pain of their rejection was precisely what guided me towards another view of healing myself and others.

Window 3: A Spiritual Model
Healing Relationships

I had removed all the alcoholics from my life and I was still hurting. I didn't know what the problem was but I knew whose problem it was. The intellectual ability, the ability to control, to analyze, to communicate, to figure things out . . . neither my mind nor my mouth had served me very well in my problem relationships. The 12-Step program introduced me to the concept of the higher power just at the time when I knew I was powerless. The third step of the 12

Steps is *"Turned my will and my life over to the care of God as I understood Him."* It was a great relief for a self-willed controller who had been trying to handle everything.

Despite my involvement in the 12-Step group, my son's drug and alcohol addiction had escalated. He was living hand to mouth on the street. I believed that he would have to get sober before we could have open and loving communication. The disease concept told me that you can't have a loving relationship with an addict because their primary relationship is with the substance. I believed that it takes two people to heal a relationship. I would work on myself until he got sober.

Now I realized that time was running out. It certainly seemed that he would die soon. I had a truly sudden and dramatic change of heart. I was no longer interested in curing his illness. I felt a great urgency to heal the relationship. I started to feel the love that had been blocked by fear, resentment and labels. I was finally able to risk telling him that I cared about him. I was no longer fearful that he could manipulate me back into rescuing him. I made a conscious decision to accept him just the way he was and to love him unconditionally. I made it okay for him to be an addict, okay for him to choose to die and I was willing to love him in that moment just the way he was . . . not if he changed or when he got off drugs.

During one of his periodic phone reports I know he heard and felt my change of heart.

"I know you are not happy with your life the way it is but I also know you have the power to change it any time you wish and I just want you to know I love you very much."

The heaviness was gone from my life. The burden lifted. I knew that my happiness was no longer dependent on his sobriety. It freed me to love him unconditionally. I believe that that was what he had wanted from me all along.

He called me three weeks later to tell me he had placed himself in a treatment center. That was five years ago and he has never had a relapse. Today he manages his own welding business in Southern California. He is sober, reasonably serene and an active gratefully recovering member of a 12-Step program.

In looking back I believe that my healing process began with the 12-Step program and was nurtured by the teachings of Jack Boland at the Unity Church of Today in Warren, Michigan. I was very much influenced by the teaching and support groups of Arnold Patent and the study of Universal Principles. I employed meditation, affirmation and creative visualization as tools to change my thinking.

I practiced seeing my son as he could be, focusing on the potential he had to heal himself. Up to that time I had reinforced the perspective of his disease, his dependency, the tragedy of his unfulfilled life. What we focus on expands. When I continue to speak of my loved ones as "sick," they will prove me right and demonstrate the accuracy of my belief. I discovered that the changes I was looking for in others required that I open up to new viewpoints. I shift my position. I change my mind. I take my consciousness up to a higher level and view the problems and the problem people from the penthouse. Insight is an inside job!

In my spiritual practice I had quieted down. The effort of the other stages where we "work" on ourselves was transformed to a much more peaceful introspective path. I gently practiced replacing images of *what was* to *what I would like to see.* From a spiritual window I could see that I must change my perception before my reality will change. From this vantage point "seeing is believing" must be cast away. In its place I practice "believing is seeing." I realize that mind creates the material expression. The vision or the idea comes before the invention. Now I practice internal positive visualization instead of manipulating an external illusion.

I have described three ways of looking at dis-ease. The process of expanded awareness has been healing for me and my family. There is no one right way to see anything. If you have a different view, do not judge that it is wrong to see it that way. Insight comes from looking through many windows. Trust that your process is the right one for you. Healing requires that you accept yourself and everyone else just where they are, letting go of the idea that any of us "should" be seeing it differently. Do not be caught up in the old belief that if you accept where you are, you'll never get out of it. Acceptance, not self-criticism, is the fertile ground from which we nurture our spiritual potential.

The return to school of my youngest child in January of 1987 meant I had made amends to and peace with all of them. John at 25 was sober in California. Anne, 22, had been out of the drug treatment center for four years, was also active in a 12-Step program. She was a junior in college, studying marketing and business. Katherine, her younger sister, was attending the same small school in Michigan and weaving back and forth between teacher training and theater studies. Their education was financed by a small trust fund from their dad.

I peeked out from behind the wall of demands and responsibilities which had boxed me into a traditional life. It looked like the coast was clear and I made my break. I resigned my corporate sales position and took myself on a 15,000-mile road trip across the Sun Belt of the United States. I called it "Time Out For Good Behavior." It was not an escape, but rather a celebration. A reward, a revival, a recreation. I combined miles of beautiful scenic driving and time alone with visiting my vast network of friends who live in various parts of the country. In my willingness to experience uncertainty and loneliness, I found that I was never lonely. The long driving time turned out to be a meditation, and I became centered in uncertainty.

Did my family and friends support this venture with great enthusiasm? Not quite. Reactions varied from inquiries as to my sanity to anger masking jealousy. My daughters who were both in college said, "Mother, we think you could have found a more convenient time to have your mid-life crisis." I knew that if I waited for permission, I would never do it. I suspected that my security did not rest on my job or my pension plan any more than it had on my marriage. There were many whispered inquiries as to the financial reserve one needs to pull off such a bold venture just when most people are thinking about saving up for their retirement. I know now what I didn't know then. Mid-life transitions require exactly as much money as you have allotted to them.

It takes every penny you have and whatever amount you have will be enough. In the process of being willing to give up what I had accumulated financially, I established a spiritual trust fund which will support me abundantly for the rest of my life!

What else did I gain? I found out some of the things I love to do when I'm not doing for everyone else. I found out that I am as good a friend to myself as I have been to others. I am good company and trustworthy. I gained a new respect for myself. I quieted down the noisy left side of my brain and listened to my creative intuitive feeling self.

What about you? You don't have to leave home to have a discovery adventure.

Ask yourself . . . .

1. How do I like to play when I'm not playing mother, career person, daughter or wife?

2. What do I like to do when I don't have to do anything?

3. What do I have when I have only me?

4. Why am I here on the planet at this time? What is my purpose in living?

What will you do for you when you are no longer doing so much for others? Here is a quick passport to a mental pleasure trip for yourself.

Begin Your Recovery From Rescuing With A Celebration Of Your Unique Life

These are 10 things I love to see:

_____
_____
_____
_____
_____

These are 10 things I love to hear:

_____
_____
_____

These are 10 things I love to touch:

These are 10 things I love to smell:

These are 10 unforgettable moments in my life:

These are 10 activities that I enjoy:

These are 10 friendships I treasure:

These are 10 things I want to do in the next 10 years:

9

Error And Amends
Who Hurts?
Who Heals?

If We Are Innocent, Why Is The "Amends" Process Part Of Spiritual Recovery?

It is my experience with the 12 Steps that the process of inventory and making amends help us to reveal our innocence to ourselves and to recognize the ultimate innocence of others. The process rids us of guilt and gifts us with responsibility instead.

I am in a family where three generations are recovering from their spiritual deprivation using a 12-Step program. I have been the giver and receiver of formal and informal, written and oral amends from several members of my family. The most curious thing I noticed was that the amend is usually for the benefit of the person making the amends, and often not of particular significance to the recipient. I smile when I think of the people who had been suffering from

guilt with things they thought had hurt me when in fact I
could hardly remember the incident they were talking about.
And I have almost never received contrite acknowledgment
from someone if I am still feeling the sting of any perceived
wound. Likewise, I just casually observed that my attempts at
formal amends to persons I thought I had harmed were met
with polite indulgence. Real relationship healing came about
from heart-felt changes deep in my soul and over time.
Words had nothing to do with it.

Recently I wrote an "amends letter" to my son. When I
wrote it, I thought it was to help him heal but it was very
helpful to me in working out my own stuff. I print it for you
here in all its revealing intimacy. You can decide whether I
am still working out my stuff at your expense or whether it
helps you get the feeling for the difference between guilt and
responsibility; between denial and awareness, between
defending my own actions and acknowledgment of everyone's feelings.

Dear John,

*"Made direct amends to those we had harmed except when
to do so would injure them or others."*

This fourth step in our 12-Step recovery program reminds
me that words are cheap, so I have preferred to work this step
by changed attitudes and actions, rather than apology for past
mistakes.

The past is gone and neither of us can change it. I have also
found that while dwelling on the past is not healing in and of
itself, repressing the emotions connected with it keeps us in
our dis-ease. As an amend to you I want you to know that
until recently I wasn't able to see your pain, your fear, your
feelings of abandonment and helplessness because I could
not confront my own. There is no defense to this fact and no
excuses to be made for it. It just is. I have forgiven myself for
the ultimate "sin" of being human, of being unable and
unwilling to open myself to giving and receiving love.

I am changed. I am open to allowing you to speak to me
of all the pain and hurt you suffered when you were a little
boy, as well as of whatever you are feeling now. You can say

anything you would like. You are free to feel all of the feelings, no matter how negative you think they are and I will love you through it. You can write or call. I would like to support you through the healing process and although I cannot change the past, I can *be there* for you now as I was not *there* for you in the past.

I remember when we brought you home from the hospital. You cried a lot for no reason. I was so sensitive to your pain and yet powerless to stop it. I didn't know what was wrong and I could not comfort you. You would stiffen up in my arms when I tried to cuddle you. I thought I was a very bad mother and felt helpless and afraid. We took you around to doctors to try and get *you* fixed. Your grandfather prescribed sedatives for your relief and ours. We thought we were doing the right thing.

If I was not able to comfort you when you were a colicky baby, I had even fewer resources to offer during your early years with two other babies and an alcoholic husband. I know that you were a battered child for in my desperation to control your uncontrollable behavior, I resorted often to physical punishment. You truly mirrored the chaos of our family, the hidden shadow of repressed anger and rage that your father and I would not face in ourselves. You were the scapegoat. We projected our angry feelings towards our parents and each other onto you. We could not see the problems between us in our marriage until you were away at military school and we no longer could blame you for the difficulty.

I remember being overwhelmed with guilt and confusion and put myself into counseling in 1967, which was the very slow beginning of being willing to face my own dragons.

Even though I knew I was part of the equation of your behavioral problems, I made the decision to put you in military school because at the time I thought I was afraid that you would hurt me or the girls permanently. You were pretty unpredictable when you were angry and we were always walking on eggs trying to prevent you from acting out your anger. I felt helpless that I couldn't physically control a nine year old, besieged by criticism from others, overcome with self-doubt and I was afraid for all of us. I now realize that I was as much afraid that I would kill you as that you would kill or injure me or the girls. You were accident prone, too. I was always waiting for the next accident to happen. I couldn't keep you safe and I felt guilty and responsible every time you got hurt. I thought you would die and it would be my fault. I wanted us both to be safe and feel safe so I sent you away.

Of course, if I wasn't facing my feelings, I never saw you express any fear, remorse or guilt at all. I just saw this tough fearless kid who moved like a tornado. I did not know enough at that time to look behind the mask of bravado to see you or myself as the frightened insecure children that we both were. For that lack of insight I am truly sorry for it caused us both much pain.

On the brighter side, it is through the pain that we begin to grow and learn and have more insight about ourselves, our parents and others in the world. We know we must look beyond the apparent circumstances and go deeper to the true meaning. The pain of making peace with your past is the healing process for your recovery and the hope of happiness in future relationships with women and the authority figures who have plagued you so.

I now see that despite the disturbing emotions and fault-finding events of the past, we have always loved each other deeply. We have repressed that too and as we recover, each in our time and in our own way, we will have many years to give expression to our love for each other.

So my dear little son, cry the tears the little boy could never cry. Feel the sadness, the anger, frustration and despair you could never feel or express when you were young. Punch the pillow, scream at the top of your lungs, kill the bad mother in your dreams. Let it out. Let it all out. Let me know how I can help you go through this as easily as possible. You must tell me what you want from me because I am not God and I don't know. Surround yourself with other supportive people who have been through this.

You don't have to be afraid any more. I'm no longer afraid of your anger or my evil shadow. There is nothing you can do or say that will keep me from loving you or loving myself. I am free and I know you soon will be too.

Feel the anger at your dad. Anger at his inability to confront his own feelings of fear and love. See how you are alike, how you mirrored each other. Perhaps one day you will see how much he loved you even though he couldn't show it. It's okay to be really mad at him for that and for dying. I hope this doesn't sound irreverent but I think his death was the event which got you sober and so I see it as the greatest gift of love he could give you.

I love you, John, and I hope you can feel the love that is there.

Mom

As I travel and talk to so many people about their emotional wounds, I see that the close-up picture I have just painted of our dysfunctional family is not so unusual after all. Part of my healing process was the willingness to question my belief in the reality of the functional family!

"A normal person is just someone you don't know very well."

Jean Houston

10

Nonjudgment
What Is The Suspended Spectator?

If you are tired of the rescuer's role, I would like to introduce you to a new character. This is a role that you can play in your own life drama and an amazingly useful role to play when others invite you into their productions. Put on the costume of the Suspended Spectator. Watch tragedy become comedy before your very eyes!! You will find that you can be involved in the action as an impartial listener and observer and be a better supporting player when you are not drawn into old emotional scripts.

Who Is The Suspended Spectator?

I call it The Impartial Observer. It is a way I take myself out of the action and the reaction. I am involved as a clairvoyant power who can see beyond the immediate circumstances. I no longer fumble with the old props . . . the rose-colored glasses of denial. Because I am not haunted by guilt and fear, I can see everything that is going on. I am involved as a listener, but I have taken the emotion out of my ears. This is the role of focused attention with emotional detachment. It is not indifference or apathy. In this role I do not need to follow a script for I have suspended my need to know the outcome. I have learned to trust the spiritual nonjudgmental process. I am playing my role in the drama and I am aware that it is a play. I see the pain but am not drawn into the suffering. I am in the world of illusion but not of it.

Is This What A Good Therapist Does?

Yes. Think of a person who has been most helpful to you in sorting out your own real life dramas. Chances are you would say this person is a good listener. And it's probably not your mother. Mothers get hooked into our stuff. Sometimes it's a therapist or a minister because they are often trained in the technique. We feel that they are on our side. They stand with us as we work on our own clarifying process. Yet we notice paradoxically that they exhibit the neutral quality of a sounding board that reflects back what we say, how we feel without the distortion of fault-finding judgment . . . of us or the other person. The impartial observer trusts that we have the capacity to figure things out for ourselves. We come away from the exchange with a greater sense of our clarity, understanding and empowerment.

How Does It Help Others When We Don't Get Emotionally Involved?

Phyllis F. says, "When I feel like I'm out of control with my emotions, I want someone around me who is emotionally stable. It gets me back on my own track."

Bob C.'s formula for giving helpful advice, "Find out what the person wants to do and give them permission to do it!"

Don Sizer, Unity Minister, says, "When you see somebody who fell into a situational or emotional mine shaft, don't jump down into the hole of negativity to pull them out. You are both likely to stay stuck. Better to lower a ladder down, so they can climb out. Another way of seeing the difference between sympathy and empathy is to recognize that the husband who takes on his wife's labor pains is not likely to be helpful in getting her swiftly to the hospital!"

How Can I Do This If I Am Emotionally Involved?

I think we become willing to suspend our emotional investment when we see that we get happier results when we do. Most of us have already practiced being a Suspended Spectator in life's *little* games . . . riding on a bus overhearing a conversation between strangers. Perhaps even in dealing with people whose judgment we trust because it matches ours.

But now it's opening night on Broadway . . . the Big Time!! If you want to be a star at this, you'll have to play the role with your children. Play to their maturity. Treat them as adults who know what they are doing. Suspend the opinion that you know what's best for them. Remind yourself that all unsolicited advice is perceived as criticism. Now listen . . . really listen. The more you are willing to give up outcomes, to reverberate their position, the more they will open up and confide in you. The more they can hear themselves, the less they will have to defend their position. At support groups we know it is not helpful to give advice. It is common for the group leader to say "Take what is useful to you and leave the rest behind." How much confidence would we instill in our teens if we practiced these principles with them?

Why Is Listening Such An Important Part Of Being A Suspended Spectator?

Jacob Weisberg, a behavioral consultant in California, conducts classes in reflective listening for families and business people. He narrates the story of a woman who was trying to tell her husband about something that was important to her. He did not appear to be listening. As a matter of fact he had his head buried in the newspaper while she was talking to him. Finally in a burst of frustration she tore the paper from his hands and said, "You haven't heard a word I said." He immediately turned to her with resolute eye contact and repeated verbatim everything she thought he had not heard. Weisberg asked his audience if they thought the woman felt better after she knew her husband had received her message. The answer, of course, is no. The point is that the *feeling of being heard is more important than actually being heard!* He describes an empathetic listening model who leans towards the person talking, makes eye contact during the communication process and invites the other party to "Tell me more!"

When we suspend our need for agreement, when we are willing to listen for understanding, when we are truly attentive not just biding time to present our side, we reap great rewards in communication. Listening becomes loving!

Isn't This A Pretty Tall Order For A Human Being?

Well, I think that's true. From my own experience becoming a detached observer is not so much a skill as a spiritual gift. While it is something we work at becoming, most of us are aware that in the end it is not something we earn but something we become open to receive. It comes to us at the most auspicious moments.

Two days after Christmas in 1983 as I was coming downstairs in my bathrobe to make the coffee I had a premonition that someone else was in the house. I rounded the corner to the den and found a strange young man standing next to the closed patio door. Although he was a total stranger, I was not frightened and instead of panic I felt a great calmness come over me. He was disoriented, appeared confused. We exchanged a few words and I quietly asked him to leave. He did not move. I did not move. I felt the event as suspended in time and was consciously aware that I was not feeling the emotion of fear that one would normally associate with such an experience. It was like watching a movie. When he did leave after a few hesitant moments, my over-riding emotion was gratitude for the gift of peacefulness we had both received.

Is It Easier To Play The Impartial Observer With Others Than With Ourselves?

If we've been in a 12-Step program, we've probably been spending quite a lot of time taking inventory. We made a list of personal debits and credits, character defects, people we had harmed, and then went to work to eliminate our faults. We hoped we could get it right the next time. When I am willing to play Suspended Spectator with myself, I choose to be peaceful rather than righteous. I see what is going on with me but give up judging it wrong to be that way. It certainly makes life more fun.

I have not been very tolerant of my ego. I held the opinion that it separated me from people and from my higher self. I tried to contain it, squash it, placate it . . . all manner of manipulative moves. When it would rise up, I would try to push it down. And just like a resistant child, it became more uncontrollable. I have learned that when I embrace it, it doesn't get out of hand nearly so often.

I recently attended a dinner-dance for an organization I have been active in for 10 years. Many people were acknowledged for their contributions to the club in the after dinner ceremony. I noticed, not impartially I might add, that my name was not mentioned. As new and old members were taking their bows, I wondered how it happened that I was left out. Had everyone forgotten that I had initiated a second group, conducted a publicity campaign, spoken of our work to outside organizations and had been a primary hot line contact for over nine years? I observed that my ego was offended but my suspended spectator danced away the evening and had a terrific time.

The next morning, however, I noticed myself licking sand-papered feelings. I began feeling self-righteous, indignant and sorry for myself. I even shed a few tears. I wanted to do something to make them go away. I thought I might call someone. Maybe I'd feel better if I was assertive about expressing my feelings. Then I asked myself what the outcome of that would be. Would I really get the feeling I wanted if I did that? I noticed that I wasn't angry at "them" for the oversight. I wasn't angry at myself for being sensitive. I wasn't chastising my ego for causing the discomfort. *I noticed that the act of observation and acceptance made the feelings disappear.* I was willing to touch myself at the feeling level. I remembered that feelings are like colors. If I do not assign a positive or negative value to them, they are free to come . . . and free to go.

A few days later I was able to see the perfection in the situation through the 11-step process which you will find in Appendix 3 of this book. It became clear that the purpose of the situation was for me to release this particular group with love. We had supported each other graciously for many years, and now it was time for me to go on to other places and for new members to carry on the tradition.

The Suspended Spectator is not trying to change the world but seeks instead to change her perception of it. The Impartial Observer does not take a position. When you take on this role, you are free from having an opinion. You are also free from having to decide an issue or take sides. Feel the truth in knowing that your opinions weigh you down, limit your ability to see and hear clearly and separate you from others. Throw the ballast of your preconceived notions overboard. Notice how much lighter you are without them. See the world from a heightened awareness. The impartial observer floats lightly and freely above the dramatic controversy. This is the gentle path to enlightened relationships with ourselves and others.

The Lotus Position

Dedicated to Anna Northrop, my Yoga teacher

Be still.
Watch silently and listen intently.
Do not be disturbed by what you see or hear.
Watch your thoughts pass through your mind.
Let them come and go like clouds passing
gently across the sky.
Make no investment in your perception.
For moment by moment each formation
    takes another shape.
There is no need to fix or change.
There is no need to analyze.
There is no need to criticize.
There is no need to figure things out.
Stay in the attentive detached present.
Observe what happens.
Be happy
Centered in uncertainty.

11

The Mirror Channel
How Can I Heal Myself And My Relationships?

What Is The Mirror Channel?

The Mirror Channel is a way of looking at life, especially at conflict, that is different from the way most of us were taught to view reality. The Mirror Channel is the one we tune in to when we see things going on that we don't like and can't change or control. We found that the programs on the Hopeless Channel, the Why Channel and the How Channel were no longer informative or entertaining. We didn't get the results we were looking for.

How Is It Different?

On these other channels we have been looking at life as if it is something that happens to us.

On the *Hopeless Channel* we spend most of our time *complaining about what happens.*

On the *Why Channel* we hope that finding the answer to the question, *"Why did this happen?"* will make us feel better. If it doesn't, we switch to the . . .

How Channel. Here we spend enormous amounts of time and energy *coping with what is happening* and trying to figure out how to *control what might happen in the future.*

On the *Mirror Channel* we see reality as if it is something we create, rather than something that happens to us.

When we observe our life situations on the Mirror Channel, we begin to see that the pictures on the screen, the experiences we have in life, are outward projections of our own inner state. They aren't random events transmitted down from a hostile satellite somewhere up in the sky. In fact, if we've been paying close attention, we often see the message in print flashing across the bottom of the screen. "The problem with your picture is not the fault of your receiver." Few of us came into life with an instruction booklet for the Mirror Channel, so we sat in front of the fuzzy picture trying to manipulate everything outside of ourselves to clear it up. Sooner or later it dawns on us that we need to focus our attention on the transmitter within.

Does This Mean That We Are Responsible For Everything That Happens To Us?

On the Mirror Channel we live in an intelligent No-Fault Universe. Its grand and purposeful design is to teach us about *itself* and our alignment or misalignment with its universal laws. It operates not on moral standards but on cause and effect.

On the Mirror Channel responsibility means the ability to respond, not blame. The primary rule for watching your life on the Mirror Channel is the willingness to view what you see without judgment of right and wrong . . . especially of yourself for having created it. Here we become willing to make mistakes, willing to learn from our mistakes, willing to let others make mistakes and willing to learn from other's mistakes. We see that we are constantly self-correcting as we learn about the Universe and our place in it. We must be impartial observers in order to become enlightened. From this higher awareness we tune into Infinite Intelligence and create a more harmonious life experience.

Who Watches The Mirror Channel?

The Mirror Channel is for all of us who are tired of viewing the world from an adversarial point of view. People who are tired of conflict. People who have given up trying to find the "right" way to live. They are people who want to become light-hearted peacemakers.

What Kind Of Soundtrack Do We Hear On The Mirror Channel?

We hear ourselves saying, "I choose to see it in a different light!" While the familiar dialogue on the other channels goes like this:

The Hopeless Channel, popular with victims, "I can't be happy unless he changes."

Intellectuals enjoy The Why Channel, "Why did this happen to me?" and they are fascinated for years with the sound of various reasonable explanations.

Controllers watch The How Channel, "How can I handle this better?" They are very involved in monitoring their responses to people and situations.

What's Wrong With, "How Can I Handle This Better?"

Nothing wrong with it. It gets people on the track of focusing on themselves, instead of the other person. It keeps a lot of therapists in business. It works for many people. But it's work. It's a struggle and often people get tired of being the only one working on the relationship. They get resentful and feel that it's a struggle to keep on coping. They're stuck because they can't see any changes in the other person.

So What's The Alternative?

The alternative is to see things differently. On the Mirror Channel we see that it is our perception of reality that creates our emotional experience with it. If we are willing to change our perception from the inside, then we can have a different result on the outside.

How Is The Picture Different?

On the Mirror Channel we see that the Universe is always in perfect order and on purpose. There are no random accidents. This Universal Intelligence loves us so much that it is a perfectly consistent and persistent parent/teacher. How else would we learn? It teaches us through cause and effect. It does not judge. It does not honor right, wrong or good intentions. It honors free choice. It is always trying to teach us about ourselves and itself. It teaches us through feelings. Therefore conflict is purposeful and on purpose. Pain is a signal that we are out of alignment with Universal Law. Seeking greater happiness is the natural tendency of life. Therefore, it is basic to move toward those things that make us feel good and to avoid those things that cause pain.

Why Not Just Leave A Problem Situation?

If we run away from a person or situation which was created to teach us something, we will just repeat the uncomfortable experience. On the Mirror Channel we know we created or attracted into our lives the perfect people and the perfect situations to teach us the lessons that we forgot we wanted to learn. We become aware that the conflict with others is a projection of our own internal conflicts and is caused by an underlying intellectual judgment about right and wrong, bad and good. We become willing to fall into harmony with the Universe by surrendering the need to be intellectually right. When we become peaceful, our emotional and physical pain leaves.

How Do You Deal With The Reality Of Problem People?

I found out that I had attracted problem people in my life so that I could learn about myself. I believe that I can't be disturbed by another person's behavior or attitude unless it reflects a secret judgment I hold about myself. The Mirror Channel presents us with three images.

1. We recognize our own attitudes and behavior but judge it bad. I know that I am annoyed with penny-pinchers because I think I should be more generous with my money.
2. It is a part of ourselves that we have chosen not to recognize. I could not see that my overly critical, demanding boss was a mirror for me until I realized that that is the way I manage myself. Another example is the statement, "My pet peeves in life are traffic jams, waiting in line and impatient people!"
3. It's a behavior or attitude we would like to express but have chosen not to because we think it's wrong to be that way. My intense irritation with my children's "irresponsible behavior" mirrored to me my unconscious desire to be free from the burden of my adult responsibilities.

How Does The Mirroring Process Change Anything?

The judgments we make about another person's condition or behavior become a two-edged sword. We attack others with our belief that they should be different and wound ourselves with the same criticism. For example:

"Joe is self destructive. He shouldn't be that way."

"Mother is going to die. She shouldn't do that."

"My boss is a very negative person and doesn't know how to manage people."

The conflict goes away when we are willing to acknowledge that these judgments reflect our own fears and feelings of powerlessness. I believe we can heal relationships only when we are willing to give up trying to change the other person's behavior or cure the other person's illness. On the Mirror Channel we take another look at the concept of constructive criticism. We see that in the nurturing soil of acceptance of self and others, people are transformed by love.

The problem people in our lives unconsciously want only one thing from us . . . acceptance of them . . . just the way they are. The unacceptable behavior will escalate until we give them what they want. The moment we give them the gift of unconditional love, we have also given it to ourselves. Unconditional love means allowing others to be just the way they are and allowing yourself to be just the way you are. This is how pain, conflict and power struggles with problem people can be removed from our lives.

What About Confronting Other People With Their Unacceptable Behavior?

There is nothing wrong with the desire to do that. It means, however, that we are not looking at life from the Mirror Channel but rather from another perspective. On the Mirror Channel we remind ourselves that all issues of unacceptable behavior are our own spiritual issues, masquerading as someone else's behavioral problems.

There is no right or wrong about confrontation. The need to confront someone else about their behavior reflects my desire to confront myself. In a behavioral context the results we get from a confrontation are always determined by the motive behind the action. And you can't fake this one. The outcome always reflects back to us whether we are looking for harmony or a fight.

When I pretend that I just want to express my honest feelings and I make the other person angry by doing so, I know that what I secretly wanted was a change in their behavior.

For example, let's say I thought it would make me feel better to talk to my husband about leaving his dirty clothes lying around the bedroom. If I stay totally focused on my own feelings with "I" messages ("When the house is messy, it makes me feel nervous"), he is not likely to be defensive and upset. He is more likely to pick up after himself than if I said, "I'm not going to be picking up after you like your mother always did."

Doesn't This Belief System Preclude The Existence Of An Objective Reality? If Everyone Creates Their Own Reality, How Do We Know What Is Real? What Is True?

How do we know what is objective reality when everything we experience comes through our five senses? The result of all we really know is what we perceive to be the truth. The Mirror Channel is like a game of inside out. We practice the opposite of seeing is believing. Wayne Dyer says start changing your belief that there are never any parking spaces when you need them. Before you get to the crowded shopping mall, begin to visualize that someone is pulling out of your "reserved space."

You activate the law of positive expectancy and watch the desired result take place. You begin to trust the truth of believing is seeing and can play the game with mastery in other more important areas of your life.

Wouldn't People Who Have A Lot Of Trouble Be The Most Reluctant To Accept That They Had Caused It All?

Yes, until they are more interested in getting rid of their pain than in holding onto ideas that cease to be useful. Mirror Channel viewing is for people who are tired of trying to figure out what's right and would prefer to concentrate on feeling better. This means that anyone can select whether or not the programs here are interesting, entertaining or informative. The Mirror Principle is not the only way to look at things. As a matter of fact most of us do quite a bit of channel-switching. But for healing the really tough repetitive situations, it certainly has worked for me.

Isn't It Pretty Egocentric, Even Blasphemous, For Us To Believe We Are The Center Of The Universe? It Sounds Like You Have Us Each Playing God As Well.

On the Mirror Channel we feel in our hearts that which our mind can't accept without a battle. We understand that acknowledging our own divinity does not mean denial of a higher power. We see that the spiritual and the human walk hand in hand. The human condition mirrors the situation of the spirit.

"Since your fundamental essence is God Energy, which is creation, you create. You are the creator. You are the creation. You create your distortions, you create your truths. This is how you learn . . . Come into life, and see it all as a wondrous and valuable learning experience. You can see within each circumstance where you have been the potter of the clay and in the outer reality of your creation you can detect the mirror image of your own self."

Emmanuel's Book
Pat Rodegast
and Judith Stanton

"I am humbled by the awareness of my own divinity. I forgive myself for so often falling short of its expression."

The Reverend Karen Boland

The following questions were submitted by participants during a workshop in Atlanta, Georgia.

As an Adult Child of an Alcoholic I'm having some trouble understanding how being unconditionally loving is different from stuffing feelings. I'm afraid if I follow your formula for healing, I'll be right back into the old trap again.

I love this question because I'm still learning the difference. The way we practice unconditional love of ourselves is by being honest about how we really feel. You make it okay to feel what you feel and you make it okay to talk about your feelings. When you don't stuff your emotions, you won't need to project blame or anger to get rid of the feelings. Then you can express yourself in "I" messages. The confrontation might go something like this:

"When you come in drunk at 2:00 a.m., it scares me to death. I wonder where you've been. Each time I think you might be with another woman, I feel that a great monster is eating me alive bit by bit. I lose another piece of what I value so much and that is the relationship we had five years ago. I remember how happy we used to be, how much we cared for each other. I miss what we had so much, that sometimes I just want to shrivel up and die. But mostly it hurts me so much, I just want to hurt you back. I love you but I see it dying and I don't know what to do about it. I feel helpless, alone and frightened. I often wonder if you feel that way, too."

Can you feel the love coming through — the honest expression of pain? This is human. This is real. This is the stuff they have been waiting to hear. There is great vulnerability here, and it is a requirement for healing . . . of ourselves and our relationships.

Maybe you have found that the unlovable characters in your life persistently test your integrity until you get honest with yourself. We can know that the ideal is to be unconditionally loving and also know that we aren't there yet. When I can accept the truth that I am angry, resentful, jealous and have negative emotions, then I no longer have to cover myself or defend my position that I am a self-righteous saint. When I am willing to present myself as I really am, I free myself and I free the other person to be who they are . . . even if they want to leave me.

Why do I have negative people in my life when everyone says I am such a positive person? What is this mirroring?

It is a very common occurrence for truth students who have recently come onto a spiritual path of positive thinking and optimistic self-enlightenment. Our negative reaction to these toxic people is judgment that they aren't enlightened, that they should be doing what we are doing. They shouldn't be negative. We are really in denial that there is a part of us that is suspicious, unloving and fearful or critical. And until we acknowledge that part of us and make it acceptable, we will be disturbed by others who act out our negativity and voice our reservations for us.

I am very disturbed by my daughter's lies. She never tells the truth. What does it mean?

It means you have an expectation of her that she is not willing to meet. It also means you are not being honest with yourself about some issue and you are angry at yourself.

Why is it that although I do know how to have fun, I most often choose not to have fun. Instead I choose to be really responsible and serious, especially at work.

I often ask myself the very same question, even though I now work for myself. I know that my feelings of urgency and demand are self-generated. Asking why is an activity for the Why Channel and, as we all know, coming up with an answer is not likely to make us feel less burdened.

On the Mirror Channel you and I can move immediately to another question, "How would I rather feel instead?" I want to feel light-hearted and peaceful. How about you?

We can both practice Arnold Patent's Three-Step Dance of Life.

The first step is *Look what I created*. Let's take the responsibility for the feeling by acknowledging that we have chosen it. (Responsibility does not mean fault. It means the ability to respond.)

The second step is *I will not judge it right or wrong*. Let's not stumble over our own feet on this one. Let's not "should on ourselves," Okay? "I *shouldn't* be feeling this, I *shouldn't* be doing this to myself," or "I *should* always be joyful at work." When we judge something, we're stuck. Let's let go of the judgment and move right on to the fun part.

The third step is *How would I rather feel instead?* Now we are free from the intellectual "shoulds" and can get right into the joyful feeling.

George Fine, a recovering intellectual from California and one of my wonderful joy teachers, says we can choose (1) not to judge a situation; (2) not to judge our feelings about a situation, and (3) not to judge our feelings about our feelings. I invite you to join me in that dance number. I guarantee it will keep us both hopping.

How can I learn how to discern what the real issue is in the mirror and what I am judging?

I say, "Wow, this doesn't feel good. I bet I think somebody or something is wrong. Guess I've been thinking judgment thoughts." The mirror is always precisely targeted on the bull's eye issue of a standard of right and wrong that we hold for others and for ourselves. A specific outward criticism of them reflects an inner attack that we are delivering simultaneously and subconsciously to ourselves.

For example, if I get upset when someone didn't appreciate my efforts to help them, I know I judge that it is impolite not to acknowledge a gift. I remind myself that a real gift is freely given solely for the pleasure that it gives me in giving it. If I choose to postpone the joy until the gift is acknowledged, then the gift was conditional. Real giving is from a heart that is free . . . and therefore not in need or wanting something in the future. The ungrateful people in my life taught me to recognize my illusions about giving. Now that I see the difference between giving unconditional gifts and making conditional business deals, I can choose which experience I would rather have. When I no longer have a hidden agenda with myself or others, I no longer attract the people or situations who will disappoint me.

Here's another example. If I feel angry that I have been manipulated or abused, I know I have a belief that it is wrong to do that. It mirrors the illusion that it is possible for one innocent party to be a victim of someone else's power. I remind myself that I am only vulnerable to manipulation or deception when I am keeping secrets from myself. Each experience I have with power struggles is a chance for me to surrender to the truth. I have chosen to believe that someone else was more powerful than me. I have handed them my power and invited them to show me the illusion of my helplessness.

Is everyone a mirror for me? How do I know?

You cannot love or hate something about another person unless it reflects to you something you love or hate or have denied about yourself. Those others reflect the part of us that (1) we recognize but judge ugly; (2) refuse to see, or (3) we secretly would like to express. When we recognize and become willing to release all judgment of them and ourselves, we no longer attract these people and these situations into our lives. One of the biggest highs you can get in life is to find that a person or situation that was previously difficult for you is still there, but you are no longer disturbed by it. You have put on the raincoat of inner serenity. And malcontent in the atmosphere just slides right off your back!

For example, perhaps I, a rather serious no-nonsense person, fell in love with and married a happy-go-lucky free spirit. Now I find that what was an attractive complement in the dating relationship causes problems for me in marriage. He's off having a fun time and I'm stuck at home with worry and responsibility. Alas! My prince has turned into a frog.

On the Mirror Channel I take 100% of the responsibility for what I see. I see that I carry a lot of ideas about duty, obligation and responsibility . . . about self-sacrifice and the work ethic. I see in my judgment that it is right to take care of business first and play later. (Or maybe never!) The Universe is always on purpose teaching us that we are here to enjoy ourselves. "Be ye as little children," commands the Bible. And those of us who like to play God by controlling everybody and everything get lots of irresponsible people around us who will act out "immaturity" until we give ourselves permission to lighten up and let go.

I feel some "heart" truth in what you are saying but my head wants to resist it. How do I work through this? How did *you* work through this?

Say, "Oh, Hi, Resistance! There you are, you devil! I recognize you. You used to be a giant dragon blocking the door to my peace of mind. But now I see you are just an innocent child wearing a fierce mask." Our resistance is nothing to be afraid of. You don't have to do battle with it or even work on it. Just love it as a perfect part of you and watch it melt away.

How did you make quantum leaps with self-love? Meditation? Therapy?

Perfect! Quantum leap in particle physics is a tiny almost infinitesimal move. And that's how I still practice learning to love myself. One step at a time, with many teachers along the way. In addition to my children, John, Anne and Katherine, who were my most effective and persistent teachers, I learned much from Jack Boland, Arnold Patent, Wayne Dyer, Ram Dass, Gerry Jampolsky, Hugh Prather, Shakti Gawain, Krishnamurti and Jean Houston, to name just a few. I've had several support groups and literally hundreds of people who loved me unconditionally, even while I was trying to change them. I had traditional therapy and nontraditional therapy. Since I was working so hard to get fixed, I wasn't a very good candidate for meditation until recently. And I found that my journey across the country alone last year was a meditation. I calmed right down. Got out of my head and into my heart. Now at least I know what it feels like, even if I can't sustain it for very long.

How can we help others (and self) to make the transition to self-love and support?

We just practice with patience. I think what we are speaks louder than what we say as a demonstration to others. On the Mirror Channel we see that we *are* others and they *are* us. Every step we take in self-love is felt by all others as love for them. We gently remind ourselves that what is good for us is good for all others. We practice being kind to ourselves. If we see someone on the outside resisting us, we know it is a part of us that is withholding love. Their resistance will signal to us that we are attached to the illusion of separateness. As my family observed me nurture myself, attend to my needs and desires, gently give voice to my feelings, I gave them permission to do the same. When I did more of what I wanted to do and less of what I thought I should be doing, I unburdened myself. The result was I was more fun to be with and had more love to give to them.

I have been an infertility patient for 10 years and am interested in how the mirror principle applies to this condition. I am a DES daughter with other complications so it is not entirely unexplained infertility.

It sounds like you've been watching the Why Channel (medical explanations) and maybe the How Channel, too (how can I cope with this?). When you switch to the Mirror Channel, you accept that it is not an accident of birth or fate that you are in this situation. You didn't specifically pinpoint the emotional distress so I will guess.

If you feel that you are missing one of life's great joys, or that you have lost something, then you may wish to release that judgment and cherish what you have. If you feel you have much unexpressed love, you could begin immediately to find children who need it. When and if you choose to see this situation as "perfect" (remember, perfect does not mean "ideal"), you will open yourself to your divine purpose and the peacefulness will come to you. You are probably already aware that giving up trying to have a baby is one of the ways people get them.

I'm slow in discovering what I really want to do (my purpose in life). How do I use the Mirror Channel to find what I want?

Give up the illusion that you are "slow" and the judgment around it. You are always on time and on purpose. Think less about what you should do. Give your attention and trust to feeling. What activities give you joy? If you can't think of anything that gives you pleasure, try new experiences. Spend time alone. Develop the gentle art of cocooning. Regenerate from within. Or do something to shake yourself out of your pattern. Take tap-dancing lessons. Join a support group. Do more of what's easy and fun. Where are your natural talents? Allow it to be perfect that you don't "know" right now. Get off your own case. Watch what comes in. On the Mirror Channel we see that from an inner state of feeling good, we can connect to a source of wisdom that will guide us to our divine purpose. You will be inspired. The word *desire* means *from the Father*.

My greatest struggle is to become totally accepting and unconditionally loving of myself. As a minister I preach this, believing it has to be true and wanting to love others this way. How can I grow in this and does it take time?

Those inside and outside of your profession believe that ministers should be totally loving and accepting of others. When you feel something other than unconditionally loving, I would suspect it causes self-judgment to pop up. Then you have a struggle on your hands. Loving ourselves unconditionally means we accept that we are human, even if we are ministers. Being human means I will not always feel loving and accepting of myself or others. Each time I am aware that I am judging and withholding love, I just notice it like an impartial observer. I see that the observation is a chance to love myself just the way I am right now. I don't have to wait until I improve. While I am loving myself as I am, I hold in mind the ideal of perfect love, perfect joy and perfect peace. I realize that it is my potential and if I had already achieved it, I would no longer need to be in my body.

How does the Mirror Principle apply when I try to separate myself from a sick (psychotic) person, and that other person continues to harass me and come back into my life?

On the Mirror Channel we see that we are not only the director of our dramas but that we have written the script and cast the leading players in their roles. The villains are our persistent teachers. They keep coming back to remind us that it is a play with a purpose. Your Mirror shows me that you choose to learn that mental illness is not a condition but an illusion. What is it exactly that disturbs you about this person and their behavior? That is the precise clue to the conflict in you. Whatever you fear from this other person is something you fear for or in yourself. Are you worried about your own potential violent or aggressive behavior? About being a little off yourself? Do you think erratic or unpredictable behavior is bad?

Give up the idea that there is something wrong with this person. See them as a perfect reflection of something you would like to reveal to yourself. Neither of you is sick. You are both innocent. When you can accept the other person just the way she is (without the negative label "sick"), then you will have received the lesson of nonjudgment that will give you the peace of mind you are seeking. Keep in mind a spiritual perspective of illness: "All sickness is homesickness!"

How do I turn a relationship around or do I just go look for another one? I have confronted him with my acceptance of him just as he is, but this has brought a more negative response. I always seem to commit to the man who cannot return the commitment.

If your perception is that your friend won't make a commitment, you know it is your own reluctance to do it. The repetitive nature of these situations is just a reflection of your own ambivalence. It makes no difference whether you leave or stay in the relationship. There's no fault in not being willing or able to commit. You have it just the way you want it at the unconscious level. The value of the Mirror Channel is that it shows us what we really want at the unconscious level, not what we think we want at the conscious level. When *you* are ready to commit, he will, or you will let go of this relationship and attract someone who will. Being aware that you are looking at your own stuff is the only way you will change your experience.

Everything, always, in my life has required me to control, and so my greatest problem is my ego and appearance of ego. Yet the Mirror Concept encourages me to see everything as a reflection of me. It seems ego-centered to believe that everything that happens has to do with me and it seems to be counter to my efforts to eliminate ego. *Help!!!*

Ego likes to set things up in either/or fashion. Either it's black or white, right or wrong. I'm in control or I'm not in control. I'm egocentric or God-centered. Patricia Sun calls this duality thinking. She says it's what happened when man ate from the tree of knowledge (judgment). The result was separation from God and "Paradise Lost." So maybe we can say that original sin, the source of our dis-ease, is thinking about things as opposites. That's just a little intellectual excursion into the Why Channel.

The Mirror Channel shows us that *you* are in conflict with *your ego.* You see them as opposing forces. You have judged that it's bad to be egocentric and you are fighting a part of yourself. But you've probably noticed that whatever you fight against, you give power to. Whenever you try to change, fight against or resist something, *it has you.* That is precisely why will power doesn't work. When we stop trying to control something, we have regained our power.

Embrace your ego. See it as self-consciousness, a perfect survival mechanism. LeShan wrote in his book on meditation that there are **three equal paths to enlightenment**:

focus on self
service to others
attention to God.

When you can observe your ego without judgment, it will no longer need to act like a willful tyrant.

I am finding it very hard to accept the irresponsibility of my children. How can I let go? How can I accept this? How can I be peaceful within?

First, *let go* of the idea that your responsibility is to teach them responsibility. On The Mirror Channel we look for the lesson they came to teach you. Perhaps the lesson you would like to learn is that you want to be more responsible for yourself. Are they acting out behavior that you would secretly like to enjoy? Are they getting high? Are they have a good time? Are they being lazy? Not working? Not earning? Maybe they're not worrying about anybody but themselves? Get the focus off the unacceptable behavior of the kids. Let them be just the way they are. You don't have to pay their bills, monitor their school work and you can't control their use of drugs or alcohol. Let them handle their own stuff.

You can focus on being responsible for enjoying your own life. Lighten up. Let go of the idea that life is a struggle. You don't have to take care of everyone else before you can take care of yourself. Get high on your own life.

I found that as soon as I started to pay attention to the neglected child in me, my irresponsible adolescent daughter took charge of her own life.

12

Surrender And Forgiveness
How Can I Learn
To Love Myself?

As I moved into my fourth year of leading *Recovery From Rescuing* Workshops, I noticed a shift in who was attending and what kinds of issues they were focused on. It was clear that the participants were reflecting my own transformation. I was attracting people who wanted to hear about spiritual solutions to psychological problems. Whereas previously I had spent half a day defining the problem, here were people who were just saying,

I know that unconditional love is the only issue.
I know that if I could love myself unconditionally, all my relationship problems would disappear.
Tell me how to love myself. I don't know how.

As much as I have read about it, listened to others talk about it and attempted to practice it myself, I found myself truly challenged to come up with a formula or a prescription.

In my typical left-brained linear thinking I wanted to give them a hand-out. I sat down at the word processor and the words SURRENDER CONTRACT punched in. Now as soon as I saw what I had written, I had to laugh at the paradox. This title is, of course, a contradiction in terms and the perfect reflection of how hard we work to let go. And how wonderfully loving it is for me to know that I am a paradox, a contradiction in terms.

I am the struggle between my left-brain linear masculine energy and my right-brained intuitive feminine essence. My days and nights are lived in delicious tension between taking charge and letting go, between being an active promoter and a passive reflector. I know that the power is in surrender and I must discipline myself like a well-trained warrior to find the peace within.

What Do I Know About Loving Myself Unconditionally?

I know that this thing we call self-esteem in psychology seems to be the key under the head of a sleeping giant that has kept us locked up in perceptual prisons of our own making. Our generation has spent lots of time and money blaming our parents. The generation before us accepted unworthiness as its birthright under the doctrine of original sin.

This I have learned!

Loving myself is not something I can learn to do, not something I earn, not a prescription to follow. It is rather a state of grace, a gift. Sometimes I have it, sometimes I don't. I cannot figure out how to get it or how to make it stay. It is not something I can go for, something I can work on, although I often do that just to pass the time. Rather, it seems to be something that comes in. Perhaps it is something I allow, something I let go of and give permission to. It is still a mystery.

I know that I could stand in front of the mirror every morning of my life and go through the new Twentieth Century Self-Esteem Litany:

"I Love Myself. I Love Myself. I Love Myself."

"Every day in every way I'm getting better and better."

And I also know that often when I least expect it, the old black raven of negative self-talk and doubt comes to sit on my shoulder for an hour or two . . . or sometimes for a day or two.

I think that feelings of unworthiness are cellular, biological, genetic, psychological, familial, planetary and universal to the human condition . . . evidence that we are cut off from our spiritual source. And I have learned I cannot fight it. The only hope is to surrender and release my creative energy for re-creation.

The Surrender Contract is for people who want to know how to do it . . . for people who know it's all just a game anyway . . . for people who know that sooner or later we all surrender with or without a contract.

SURRENDER CONTRACT

On this day of _____ in the year _____ I became willing to surrender my belief in my unworthiness. From this day forward I will allow the Universe to send me all of the joy, peace and happiness that I was created to enjoy. I realize that my unhappiness has been created from my misperceptions and I now become willing to let go of old ideas and see things in a new light.

_____

(Your Signature)

On the following pages you will find suggested steps that will help you love yourself and a place for personal notes as you go through the process.

I let go and release resentments of all those people who I believe have harmed me or someone else in some manner. I will list each one and forgive them and myself for my misperception. I affirm that we are all innocent.

_____

_____

_____

_____

_____

_____

_____

_____

_____

_____

I let go and release all beliefs that I have injured others by something I have done or not done. I will list each one and forgive myself for my misperceptions. I affirm that I am innocent of wrong-doing. I know that this awareness will lead me to love myself and others more.

_____

_____

_____

_____

_____

I surrender my belief that I need to feel guilt or pain in order to grow in love and spiritual awareness.

I trust my body and heart to tell me how to love myself.

_____

_____

_____

_____

_____

_____

_____

_____

_____

I will allow a support group to come into my life.

_____

_____

_____

_____

_____

_____

_____

_____

_____

_____

_____

_____

I will allow 20 minutes of quiet time each day to listen to myself. I remember that listening is loving.

_____

_____

_____

_____

_____

_____

_____

_____

_____

_____

_____

_____

_____

_____

I will allow myself to experience **all** of my feelings. I will love each of them as they come up, and I will love myself as I experience them. I let go and release judgment about my feelings.

_____

_____

_____

_____

_____

_____

_____

_____

_____

_____

_____

_____

I will be attentive to myself. I surrender my belief that I can have what I want at someone's expense. I will focus on the certainty that when I am taking care of myself, I am automatically taking care of others.

_____

_____

_____

_____

_____

_____

_____

_____

_____

_____

_____

I let go and release my belief that I must make things happen. I relax my desire to control and watch how I attract the experiences, people and feelings I desire to have. I let Universal Energy do the job for me. I release my belief in hard work and struggle.

_____

_____

_____

_____

_____

_____

_____

_____

_____

_____

_____

_____

I become willing to gently and easily surrender my use of
mind-altering substances, whether it is alcohol, nicotine,
sugar or worry. I know that my recovery depends upon being
aware and awake. I choose not to anesthetize myself from
myself. I fill up the emptiness inside me with a conscious
contact with the peace and joy of the higher power in me.

_____

_____

_____

_____

_____

_____

_____

_____

_____

_____

_____

_____

13

Alcoholism And Spirituality
Alcoholism As A Metaphor?

"Alcoholism is a physical, mental and spiritual disease."

Alcoholics Anonymous

"Alcoholism is a dis-ease of the closed heart."

Stu M.

"Alcoholism is a metaphor."

Jackie Castine

What Do You Mean By Alcoholism Is A Metaphor?

A metaphor is a literary figure of speech used to make comparisons. It is a way of explaining complicated ideas in simple imagery. The parables in the Bible are metaphorical. They are the methods Jesus used to teach simple people universal truths. For example, the story of the prodigal son describes a literal event in which an errant son was welcomed home by his father. It also describes the relationship of abundant forgiveness which is available to us from our heavenly father if we wish to return home. There are many levels of insight and wisdom in these stories. The more willing we are to see beyond the obvious literal truth, the more we expand our conscious awareness. This does not mean that what we used to believe is now false and must be negated. It just means that we now see more.

How Does That Relate To Alcoholism?

The belief that alcoholism is a physical disease . . . that people are predisposed to it by their genetic package . . . is like taking the Bible literally. (And hasn't there been as much divergent opinion about the disease concept as there has been about interpretation of the scriptures?) It explains that substance abuse is not a matter of willpower or a moral issue. But it doesn't tell the whole story. When we look deeper, we see that there are psychological factors and family dynamics which play a part in the dis-ease. And when we look even further, we become aware that there is no healing without a change in thinking. That is, we can remove the alcohol and still have the dis-ease, the "ism." As we abstract the literal truth of recovery, we see that sobriety is the vehicle, serenity the path we want and that spiritual principles provide the energy to make it work.

How Does It Help The Alcoholic And Our Society To View Alcoholism As A Metaphor?

We used to see drunks, now we see drinking problems. Are we ready for another new view? What would happen in homes, jails and hospitals if we started treating drug and alcohol abusers as highly evolved spiritual creatures. Like the disguised Princess in the story, *The Princess and the Pea,* perhaps these people are the sensitive ones whose "dis-ease" mirrors for all of us the acute pain we feel when we are emotionally separated from each other and spiritually separated from our Creator.

Alcohol is a Greek word meaning "spiritus." Liquor is spirits. Who doesn't want to be in high spirits? Are drug abusers and alcoholics any different from the rest of us who use cigarettes, food, sex, money, or work to produce euphoria and anesthesia from our wounded souls.

There are many ways to reconnect with spirit. The 12-Step program works just fine. So do churches and other support groups. Impatient alcoholics and our impetuous youth prove daily that dying is the fastest way to return to the embrace of the Creator. Some of us found ourselves reconnected with a personal God precisely because we discovered our power-lessness over the drug or alcohol abuse of someone we loved.

Alcoholism is a purposeful and powerful vehicle to lead individuals and families towards spiritual awareness and a new sense of community through the support group process. We now know that if we do battle against drugs and alcohol, we are simply attacking the messenger without attending to the message it carries.

What Is The Message In The Metaphor?

The message is that alcoholism is a gift . . . to individuals, to society and to the planet. It is a way to get spiritual. The world is becoming aware that political and economic policies have not given us solutions to the ills of the world. The healing must take place in attitude. We must change our minds if we are to change the world. The next evolutionary leap is towards higher consciousness. If we are to survive as a species, we must begin to see our oneness.

Our children's need to escape from the world's reality is a signal that we must change the world. Instead of criticizing them, we need to listen to them. We have been so distracted with our own addictions to money and power that it took a drug problem of national epidemic proportion to get our attention.

Through this dis-ease hundreds of thousands of people, young and old, are healing themselves in spiritual support groups. We, who have experienced the healing of our internal conflicts, found peace and harmony in family relationships, can use this awareness to heal the pain of poverty, dis-ease and isolation on our planet.

It will be a ministry of consciousness. A program of attraction, not promotion. There will be no rescuing, no sense of urgency about this mission. This is a program of being, not doing. We minister by example. We are willing to listen, to see similarity instead of differences. We focus on cooperation instead of competition, at home and at work. Everywhere we go we are able to duplicate the miracles we experienced at tables where strangers turned into lovers through the art of self-revelation. We cut through the illusion of age, race, color, religion and divergent points of view. We are willing to relinquish our ego's desire to be right. In the microcosm of our personal life we make a decision to be peaceful and happy one day at a time.

Appendix 1

Support Groups For Rescuers

Families Anonymous is a fellowship of people whose lives have been affected by the use of mind-altering substances or related behavioral problems of a relative or friend. Any concerned person is encouraged to attend even if there is only a suspicion of a problem. Here the emotionally involved family can find help, even if the offending member is not yet ready to seek help. Freedom from guilt, worry and hopelessness comes from listening to those who have shared similar experiences and found some answers. By attending meetings, studying the literature, talking to other members, and working the Steps of the program, the situation suddenly or gradually looks different. Reactions begin to change. Members learn to face reality with comfort, emotional growth takes place and an atmosphere of recovery is created.

Families Anonymous
P.O. Box 528
Van Nuys, California 91408
(213) 989-7841

Al-Anon Family group membership is open to all who have a close relationship to, or love for an alcoholic. The group purpose is to (1) develop intelligent understanding of the alcoholism, (2) to live according to the principles of AA in order to acquire serenity, (3) to meet regularly for the exchange of ideas and inspiration and to gain strength through prayer and meditation, (4) to practice humility and tolerance in our daily living and (5) to welcome and encourage the family of the alcoholic to participate in the program and live more abundantly.

Al-Anon Family Groups
P.O. Box 182, Madison Square Station
New York, New York 10010

Adult Children of Alcoholics is a 12-Step fellowship for men and women who grew up in alcoholic or dysfunctional families. Members identify with fear of authority, approval-seeking behavior, relationships based on helping and seeking victims, an overdeveloped sense of responsibility and inability to feel and express feelings. The solution is to keep the focus on yourself, free yourself from the past, take responsibility for your own life and become your own loving parent. This is a spiritual program based on action coming from love that allows its members to restructure their thinking and heal themselves.

Adult Children of Alcoholics
Central Service Board
Interim World Service Organization
P.O. Box 3216
2522 W. Sepulveda Blvd., #200
Torrance, California 90505
(213) 534-1815

The following are resources for finding and forming mutual aid self-help support groups.

National Alliance of Self Help (SHALL)
This is a newly formed national coalition (also acting as a clearing house) for independent self-help groups. It is a non-profit organization of self-help groups and self-helpers dedicated to supporting and promoting the principles, priorities and philosophy of self-help as a tool of empowerment.

Contact:
Lee Miller
68-27 Yellowstone Blvd., Apt. C-41
Forest Hills, New York 11375
(718) 793-1243

Hetty Hubbard, Director
Self-Help Public Health Administration Initiative
Parklawn Bldg. 6-40
5600 Fishers Lane
Rockville, Maryland 20857
(301) 443-2370

To obtain a copy of the *National Self-Help Source Book* send $8.00 to:

Ed Madera, Director
New Jersey Self-Help Clearing House
c/o St. Clare's Riverside Medical Center
Daville, New Jersey 07834

Universal Principles Support Groups (Based on Arnold Patent's book *You Can Have It All* and regional Celebration of Abundance Workshops.)

The purpose of these groups is to experience unconditional love and support, peace, harmony and abundance in all relationships.

Contact:
East
Katharine Deleot
1466 Leafmore Place
Decatur, Georgia 30033
(404) 633-0915

West
Bea Barabas
P.O. Box 8425
San Diego, CA 92104

Co-dependents Anonymous Central
P.O. Box 5508
Glendale, Arizona 85312-5508
(602) 944-0141

Appendix 2

The Twelve-Step Program

The First Step Of Alcoholics Anonymous and Al-Anon

We admitted we were powerless over alcohol and that our lives had become unmanageable.

The First Step For Adult Children of Alcoholics

We admitted we were powerless over the effects of alcoholism — that our lives had become unmanageable.

The First Step For Families Anonymous

We admitted we were powerless over drugs and alcohol and other people's lives and that our lives had become unmanageable.

Step Two

Came to believe that a Power greater than ourselves could restore us to sanity.

Step Three

Made a decision to turn our will and our lives over to the care of God as we understood Him.

Step Four

Made a searching and fearless moral inventory of ourselves.

Step Five

Admitted to God, to ourselves and to another human being the exact nature of our wrongs.

Step Six

We are entirely ready to have God remove all these defects of character.

Step Seven

Humbly asked Him to remove our shortcomings.

Step Eight

Made a list of all persons we had harmed, and became willing to make amends to them all.

Step Nine

Made direct amends to such people wherever possible, except when to do so would injure them or others.

Step Ten

Continued to take personal inventory and, when we were wrong, promptly admitted it.

Step Eleven

Sought through prayer and meditation to improve our conscious contact with God as we understood Him, praying only for knowledge of His will for us and for the power to carry that out.

Step Twelve

Having had a spiritual awakening as the result of these steps, we tried to carry this message to others and to practice these principles in all our affairs.

Appendix 3

The Eleven Steps

The following material comes from the Arnold Patent's book, You Can Have It All, *and is practiced by the Celebration of Abundance Support Group Network.*

(A Method for making the best of any situation)

1. Define the "situation."
2. Close your eyes and become aware of the feeling in your body separate from any thoughts you may have about it.
3. Are you willing to take total responsibility for all aspects of the situation? Please explain.
4. Do you agree that nothing you or anyone else has done or is doing is either wrong or right? Do you wish to share an example?
5. Perceive the situation differently. Create another interpretation of it.
6. Do you realize that you are receiving exactly what you want and the other person(s) is receiving exactly what he or she wants?
7. Do you recognize that however you see the other person is really the way you see yourself?
8. Do you realize that what you are experiencing is precisely how you see the situation?
9. Are you willing to describe the ways you are withholding love from yourself and others?

10. Go behind the apparent circumstances of the situation and locate the love in yourself and in all others involved in the situation.
11. Feel the joy that comes when the love is found and expressed.

The following is a parody of the *Eleven Steps* and I gratefully acknowledge Steven Kvaal and his support group partners from St. Paul, Minnesota: James, Nan, Tony, Helen, Deborah, Peter and Beth for their wisdom and humor.

The Eleven Stumbles

(A Method for making the worst of any situation)
1. Deny the situation.
2. Close your eyes and become aware of the feeling in your body — wallow in it. Indicate when the discomfort becomes excruciating.
3. Are you willing to blame everyone else for all aspects of the situation? Name names.
4. Do you agree that nothing you have done is wrong and that nothing anyone else had done or is doing is right? Please rationalize.
5. Perceive the situation again. Create another emotional scar.
6. Do you realize that you are getting screwed and the other person is loving every minute of it?
7. Do you realize that seeing the other person as a reflection of yourself will only make you look bad? Do you wish to blame your mother?
8. Do you realize that what you're experiencing is really worse than you think and that nobody cares?
9. Please describe the ways you've been emotionally vandalized by yourself and others and what you're going to do to get even.
10. Go behind the apparent circumstances of the situation and locate the terror in yourself and all others involved.
11. Feel the intense fear and pain that comes when terror is found and expressed.

Appendix 4

Eight Steps Into The Master Mind Consciousness

1. I SURRENDER

I, _____, surrender to the highest energy, the Hallowed Spirit within me and in the Universe.

2. I KNOW

I now know that the power of the Infinite Creative Intelligence — The Master Mind — is always responding to me in a personal way.

3. I UNDERSTAND

I now understand that aligning myself with the perfection of the Universe is the only way my life can be transformed.

4. I DECIDE

I now formally choose to align my thinking and actions with the Universe, surrendering all illusions, my will and false beliefs, and ask to be changed at depth.

5. I FORGIVE

I formally choose to forgive myself for all misperceptions I have made. I also forgive and release everyone who I perceive has injured or harmed me in any way whatsoever, and they forgive me. I know and appreciate their acting out for me what I may choose to change in myself. They are only a reflection of me.

6. I CHOOSE

I now choose health, happiness, harmony, prosperity, perfect expression of my purpose, and total well-being for myself and all others. I now make known my specific purpose and desire(s) to my Master Mind Partners, asking the Master Mind to fulfill these requests.

7. GRATEFULLY ACCEPTING

I am now living the ideal high quality life. I now experience the love and joy within me and in all others in the Universe. I joyously give thanks for Oneness with the miracle-working power of the Master Mind as a natural state of my being.

8. DEDICATION AND COVENANT

I now have a Covenant in which it is agreed that the Master Mind shall continue to supply me with an abundance of all things necessary to live a success-filled and happy life, so long as I remain an open channel of its will. I dedicate myself 100% to the expression of my purpose. I am doing that which I enjoy, being of maximum service and support to my fellow man. I am living in a manner that is ideal, setting the highest example for others to follow. I now go out into my world with a spirit of enthusiasm, excitement, expectancy and acceptance of the best. I am at peace.

John Boland,
Minister,
The Church of Today,
Warren, Michigan

Appendix 5

Life Lessons

1. **You will receive a body and a family.** You may like them or hate them, but they will be yours for the entire period of this time around.
2. **You will learn lessons.** You are enrolled in a full-time informal school called life. Each day in this school you will have the opportunity to learn lessons. You may like the lessons or think them irrelevant and stupid.
3. **There are no mistakes, only lessons.** Growth is a process of trial and error: experimentation. The "failed" experiments are as much a part of the process as the experiment that ultimately "works."
4. **A lesson is repeated until learned.** A lesson will be presented to you in various forms until you have learned it. When you have learned it, you can then go on to the next lesson.
5. **Learning lessons does not end.** There is no part of life that does not contain its lessons. If you are alive, there are lessons to be learned.
6. **"There" is no better than "here."** When your "there" has become a "here" you will simply obtain another "there" that will again look better than "here."
7. **Others are merely mirrors of you.** You cannot love or hate something about another person unless it reflects to you something you love or hate about yourself.

8. **What you make of your life is up to you.** You have all
   the tools and resources you need, what you do with
   them is up to you. The choice is yours.
9. **Your answers lie inside you.** The answers to life's
   questions lie inside you. All you need to do is look,
   listen and trust.
10. **You will forget all this!**

Author Unknown

Appendix 6

The Willingness Steps

1. Realize that as long as you are trying to change, avoid or get out of an uncomfortable experience, you will never be free of the discomfort.

2. Remind yourself that whatever you are uncomfortable about experiencing will continue to occur in your life until you are willing to have that exact experience — until you are willing to experience the exact thoughts, feelings and perceptions you are having, including any protest of the experience itself.

3. Remind yourself that when you cannot simply create something more wonderful to experience, your freedom and joyfulness ultimately depend upon your willingness to experience exactly what you are experiencing.

4. Realize that getting into the experience, not getting out of it, is the more rewarding thing to do as it is the way to master life.

From *The Truth Of Happiness*
by George Fine

Bibliography And Recommended Reading

A Course In Miracles. Farmingdale, New York: Foundation for Inner Peace, 1975.

Al-Anon. *Twelve Steps Twelve Traditions.* New York: Al-Anon Family Group Headquarters, 1981.

Bellah, Robert. *Habits Of The Heart.* New York: Harper & Row, 1985.

Black, Claudia. *It Will Never Happen To Me.* Denver: M.A.C., 1981.

Bloomfield, Harold H., and Kory, Robert B. *Inner Joy.* New York: Jove Books, 1980.

Booth, Father Leo. *Spirituality And Recovery.* Deerfield Beach, Florida: Health Communications, 1985.

Branden, Nathaniel. *Honoring The Self.* New York: Bantam Books, 1983.

Coit, Lee. *Listening.* Wildomar, California: Breezes Of Joy Foundation, 1985.

Collins, Vincent. *Me, Myself And You.* St. Meinrad, Indiana: Abbey Press, 1969.

Cousins, Norman. *The Healing Heart.* New York: Norton, 1983.

Dass, Ram, and Gorman, Paul. *How Can I Help?* New York: Alfred A. Knopf, 1985.

Dyer, Dr. Wayne. *Your Erroneous Zones.* New York: Avon Books, 1976.

Ellis, Albert, and Harper, Robert. *A New Guide To Rational Living.* Hollywood, California: Wilshire Books, 1975.

Ellis, Dan. *Growing Up Stoned: Coming To Terms With Teenage Drug Abuse.* Deerfield Beach, Florida: Health Communications, 1986.

111

Ferguson, Marilyn. *The Aquarian Conspiracy.* Los Angeles: Tarcher, 1980.

Fine, George. *The Truth Of Happiness.* Bothell, Washington, 1986.

Fishel, Ruth. *The Journey Within: A Spiritual Path To Recovery,* 1987. *Learning To Live In The Now: 6 Week Personal Plan To Recovery,* 1988. *Time For Joy Daily Affirmations.* Deerfield Beach, Florida: Health Communications, 1988.

Gawain, Shakti. *Creative Visualization,* 1978. *Living In The Light.* San Rafael, California: Whatever Publishing, 1986.

Golas, Thaddeus. *The Lazy Man's Guide To Enlightenment.* New York: Bantam Books, 1971.

Hay, Louise, *You Can Heal Your Life.* Santa Monica, California: Hay House, 1984.

Jampolsky, Gerald G. *Love Is Letting Go Of Fear,* 1970. *Teach Only Love.* New York: Bantam Books, 1983.

Johnston, E. D. *A Guide To Feeling Good.* Greshman, Oregon: Acorn Endeavors, 1986.

Keyes, Ken Jr. *The Hundredth Monkey,* 1982. *Conscious Person's Guide To Relationships.* Coos Bay, Oregon: Vision Books, 1979.

Krishnamurti, J. *The Awakening Of Intelligence.* New York: Avon Books, 1973.

Krishnamurti, J. *You Are The World.* New York: Harper & Row, 1972.

Kushner, Harold S. *When Bad Things Happen To Good People.* New York: Schocken Books, 1981.

LeShan, Eda. *The Wonderful Crisis Of Middle Age.* New York: Warner Communications, 1973.

LeShan, Lawrence. *How To Meditate.* New York: Bantam Books, 1974.

MacLaine, Shirley. *Out On A Limb.* New York: Bantam, 1983.

Mandel, Bob. *Open Heart Therapy.* Berkeley, California: Celestial Arts, 1984.

May, Rollo. *Freedom And Destiny,* 1981. *The Discovery Of Being.* New York: W.W. Norton, 1983.

Millman, Dan. *Way Of The Peaceful Warrior.* Tiburon, California: H. J. Kramer, 1980.

Newman, Mildred, and Berkowitz, Bernard. *Reconciliations.* New York: Berkley Books, 1980.

Norwood, Robin. *Women Who Love Too Much.* New York: Pocket Books, 1985.

O'Gorman, Patricia, and Oliver-Diaz, Philip. *12-Steps To Self-Parenting.* Deerfield Beach, Florida: Health Communications, 1988.

Patent, Arnold. *You Can Have It All.* Piermont, New York: Money Mastery, 1984.

Paul, Jordan, and Paul, Margaret. *Do I Have To Give Up Me To Be Loved By You?* Minneapolis: CompCare Publications, 1983.

Peale, Norman Vincent. *Positive Imaging.* Old Tappan, New Jersey: Fleming H. Revell, 1982.

Peele, Stanton. *Love And Addiction.* New York: Signet Books, 1975.

Peck, M. Scott. *The Road Less Traveled.* New York: Simon & Schuster, 1978.

Prather, Hugh. *Notes To Myself.* New York: Bantam Books, 1970.

Prather, Hugh. *There Is A Place Where You Are Not Alone.* Garden City, New York: Doubleday, 1980.

Ray, Sondra. *Loving Relationships.* Berkeley, California: Celestial Arts, 1980.

Rodegast, Pat, and Stanton, Judith. *Emmanuel's Book.* New York: Bantam Books, 1985.

Schaef, Anne Wilson. *Misunderstood-Mistreated.* San Francisco: Harper & Row, 1986.

Schaef, Anne Wilson. *Women's Reality.* Minneapolis: Winston Press, 1981.

Stearns, Ann Kaiser. *Living Through Personal Crisis.* Chicago: Thomas More Press, 1984.

Tzu, Lao. *The Way Of Life.* New York: Mentor, 1955.

Weinberg, John R., and Kosloske, Daryl. *Journey Into Growth.* Minneapolis: CompCare, 1977.

Whitfield, Charles L. *Healing The Child Within.* Deerfield Beach, Florida: Health Communications, 1987.

Wholey, Dennis. *Discovering Happiness.* New York: Avon Books, 1978.

Woititz, Janet. *Adult Children Of Alcoholics.* Deerfield Beach, Florida: Health Communications, 1983.

York, Phyllis, and York, David. *Toughlove.* New York: Bantam Books, 1982.